MUSES NO MORE

MUSES NO MORE
PORTRAITS OF OCCULT WOMEN

ÙNA MARIA BLYTH

Edited by **KAZIm**

Illustrations by **Luciana Lupe Vasconcelos**

ISBN : 978-2-492143-10-6

© Hexen Press

All rights reserved.

No part of this publication may be reproduced or transmitted in any form or by any means, electronic or mechanical, including photocopy or any storage and retrieval system, without permission in writing from the publisher.

WWW.HEXEN.FR

CONTENTS

Introduction - 9

SECTION ONE: PORTRAITS

Chapter 1 - Margot Adler: Journalist Priestess - *17*

Chapter 2 - Doreen Valiente: Mother of Modern Witchcraft - *25*

Chapter 3 - Marjorie Cameron: Muse No More - *33*

Chapter 4 - Sybil Leek: Witch Next Door - *43*

Chapter 5 - Madeline Montalban: Lady of Lucifer - *49*

Chapter 6 - Rosaleen Norton: The Witch of King's Cross - *59*

Chapter 7 - Mirra Alfassa: The Mother - *67*

Chapter 8 - Maya Deren: Sorceress of the Screen - *77*

Chapter 9 - Pamela Colman Smith: Tarot's High Priestess - *87*

Chapter 10 - Maria de Naglowska: Satanic Woman - *93*

Chapter 11 - Annie Besant: Sceptical Seeker - *101*

Chapter 12 - Leila Waddell: Rag-Time Revolutionary - *109*

Chapter 13 - Moina Mathers: A Subversive Wife - *117*

Chapter 14 - Sojourner Truth: Power in Forgiveness - *125*

Chapter 15 - Marie Laveau: Voodoo Queen of New Orleans - *133*

Chapter 16 - Biddy Early: Medicine Woman - *141*

Chapter 17 - Isobel Gowdie: The Confessor - *149*

SECTION TWO: PRACTICES

Banishing the Hungry Ghost · *159*

The Practice of Oomancy · *160*

Kinship Candle Ritual · *162*

Zodiacal Mind Training · *164*

Unglamouring Ritual · *166*

A Simple Sabbath Unguent · *168*

The Arrival Exercise · *170*

A Beginner's Guide to Possession · *172*

Tarot for Creative Blocks · *173*

Your Ears Can Be Microphones · *175*

Hexing 101: Know Your Enemy · *177*

Scrying Musical Notation · *179*

A Practice for Life · *180*

Ritual Towards Liberation · *181*

Ancestral Altar in a Box · *183*

Eyebright Tea · *184*

Witch Bottle for Bravery · *185*

Bibliography · *189*

Acknowledgements · *203*

Dedicated to the spirits of the seventeen women herein

INTRODUCTION

It began with Lilith. As a young woman I lived in London's Soho, above a pub I worked in called the Glasshouse Stores; a refuge for old timers who abhorred and detested the neighbourhood's rapidly encroaching gentrification. My shared bedsit, riddled with cockroaches and mice (an origin story would not be complete without rodents), overlooked a dank courtyard frequented by sex workers and muggers and lost drunks bound for mishap. During the day it was just another smoking area for our punters, but at night the conviviality leached down the drains and this dark hovel (a shopping quarter in the present day) became something altogether more dangerous. Bad things happened below my creaky bedroom window. I feared for the sex workers' safety. I feared for the safety of all women.

And so, to cut a very long story short, I became Lilith. That is to say, I began, very suddenly, to embody her archetype. Some might call it possession. Only, initially, I knew nothing about Lilith. Or spirit possession. It was kind of like… I became possessed and Googled what was wrong with me and it turned out I was possessed. The internet intimated that the spirit living through my body was Lilith. I prayed for those sex workers. Indeed, I dedicated a public ritual to igniting their protection, performed at St Gabriel's Hall in Pimlico that winter under the auspices of a theatrical show.

Lilith was like gasoline to my inner fire and rage and fear. I looked in the mirror and didn't recognise this bold new face slyly jeering at me. This was terrifying, of course. Thrilling? Naturally. The whole thing didn't last long; it was more of an acute than chronic possession situation. But something had shifted and my fingertips buzzed & hummed. I was ready to scrabble around.

MUSES NO MORE: PORTRAITS OF OCCULT WOMEN

And so I began my career in the occult. Don't all of our stories begin with a haphazard possession?

First stop, Watkins Books, second stop Treadwells, third stop Atlantis Bookshop. I marched up and down Charing Cross Road every day on missions to fill my head with books, marvellous books, spooky books! And alas, not only were they mostly about men, they were written by men too. I studied Aleister Crowley, Kenneth Grant, Peter Carroll, Eliphas Lévi, Gary Lachman. It was only years later, and hundreds of books in, that I noticed the dominance of these men in a world where folks who were *not men* existed too. I learned names like Doreen Valiente, Annie Besant, Marie Laveau.

This book aims to fill a gap in occult literature. Consider it a compendium of sorts. Above all, I have attempted to channel the spirits of women whose voices have often been silenced or ignored; their stories left untold or forgotten. This body of research has been a gift to me. I hope the reading of it will be gift-like to you. It is by no means definitive, but hopefully it is a start.

I also hope that a few things will become clear. Firstly, the fact that there is no one true "feminine" magic. Secondly, the fact that in delving deeply into history we face wading through a vast field of biological essentialism. Men behave in *x* way and women behave in *y* way. Women have vaginas and men penetrate those vaginas. *Et cetera*. I would like to throw all of that out the window, and indeed so too would many of the (often queer) women this book explores. In writing and reading about occult history we must, out of necessity, engage with the spectres of Western esotericism. There is a great deal of deadweight in our closets.

I would like to say that this book is a pure, unbridled celebration of women occultists, but to do so would massively fail to acknowledge the complexities of these women's lives and ideas. Indeed, some rather famous figures have been omitted from this text because, put simply, channelling their spirits made me sick. Dion Fortune's racism, for example, put me in bed for a fortnight before I scrapped her chapter. Some folks just don't deserve that kind of word count. As contemporary occultists, we can only take steps forward towards greater justice in the world if we are willing to scrutinise our histories without putting our forebears on pedestals, or hiding them in the closet because aspects of them make us too uncomfortable to dive deeply into their stories.

Many of our esoteric ancestors held very progressive beliefs. Just as many of them held deeply problematic ones. Let us consider Fortune. The 20th century's greatest female occultist, or a bigot with a homophobic and racist ideology? Can both things be true at the same time, or not? Our occult histories are often lacking in depth, nuance and an acknowledgement of the complexities of both individual occultists and their communities.

The roots of our ideologies are threaded throughout what we do now and what we take into the future. History matters. It behooves us to look into how deeply entangled problematic ideas held by individuals and communities are in the threads of their occult thinking and work. I personally do not believe the two can be separated. The person and/or the community begets the magic. The magic begets the world.

Onto another matter now. Let's call it "The Problem of Crowley." Many of the women in this book have connections with the Great Beast, Aleister Crowley. If I wasn't careful, this book could easily have turned out to be about him. But exploring his appearances more deeply, other themes began to rear their heads. Let us look at the case of Sybil Leek. As with many stories of European witches, Aleister Crowley creeps into this one too. Although never mentioned in any of Crowley's extensive diaries, Leek claimed to have met him for the first time at the age of eight. Not only did she apparently learn about poetry from him whilst climbing mountains; he even prophesied that Leek would follow in his occult footsteps, telling her grandmother:

MUSES NO MORE: PORTRAITS OF OCCULT WOMEN

> *'This is the one who will take up where I left off...You'll hear all sorts of things said about me and they'll say the same things about you, but I shall have broken the ground for you.'*

Whether Crowley said this or not is up for debate, yet there is a ring of truth in this statement: like him, Leek would be hounded, bad-mouthed, ridiculed and even feared. As a hereditary witch, Leek revered the Old Ways, and drew a sharp moral distinction between certain practices, claiming that Crowley "forgot about love and concentrated only on magic. I cannot see one without the other".

Leek was not unlike many witches and magical folk of her time: a commentary on Crowley simply had to exist. At first I thought that perhaps all roads lead to Crowley and this made me very miserable indeed, given this book's intentions. But delving deeper, it dawned on me that at Leek's time of writing the Witchcraft Act, which outlawed all forms of witchcraft in Britain, had just been repealed. In a flash I understood that maybe it was necessary for witches to comment on Crowley in order to distance themselves from him, the most famous and feared magician in the country. Perhaps, I might add more sceptically, to boost their own profiles too. Crowley was, in the public consciousness, a threat. Tabloids thrived on his image. The epitome of "black magic" revealed before their eyes. It was a dangerous time to engage with the occult.

Indeed, we see several disses of Crowley throughout this book. Madeline Montalban's origin story can be viewed as a way to demonstrate Crowley's hunger for money, for example. The truth of that particular tale - a young Montalban packed off to Crowley's house with a cheque in hand, by her disgruntled father - is debatable. But as Montalban adopted a Hermetic teaching style with her students, we can see how it may have proliferated as a cautionary tale. Crowley appears in many other stories in these pages. In some cases I decided to leave out his more minor appearances because they felt very much like old notes in a margin that no longer make sense even to the writer of them. And so The Problem of Crowley is not quite solved, but was, at least for me, loosened up in a satisfying way.

You will find that the book is divided into two sections: *Portraits* and *Practices*. Section One features biographies of the seventeen women, from the most recent death - that of Margot Adler - to the most ancient death, of Isobel Gowdie. As I have said, these portraits are by no means definitive, but I hope they give you a flavour to work with and ideas to chew on. Section Two consists of seventeen rituals I have channelled directly from the spirit of each woman. I have considered writing about my methods but, in the manner of my elementary training in trolldom, I concluded that some things are best kept secret. Perhaps if I meet you one rainy night in Soho, drinking tonic water at the Glasshouse Stores' bar, I'll whisper some in your ear.

Ùna Maria Blyth
Shetland Islands, August 2023.

Section One

Portraits

Margot Adler as High Priestess (n.d.)

Chapter One

Margot Adler
Journalist Priestess
(d. 2014)

'I guess the bottom line is that I think the intellectual level of stuff in the Craft is really poor, that people [...] become so interested in their little publications, their study of tarot, their study of this, their study of that, that they haven't really enlarged themselves.'

~ Interview with Margot Adler in
FireHeart magazine, 1990.

𝕴n 1975 Margot Adler, a young journalist working in public radio, was introduced to her boyfriend's literary agent at a bar. Over a few beers she paved the way for an eventual book deal which would change the course of public attitudes towards witchcraft on a vast scale. Published in 1979, *Drawing Down the Moon* engaged critically with modern Paganism in the United States - Wicca ('the Craft') in particular - charting it's tangled roots whilst smashing stereotypes about who Neopagans are and what they do; demonstrating the diversity of emerging nature religions, along with the lives of those who practise them. What remains most impressive about the text is not just the depth and breadth of its research, but the rigour and incision of Adler's intellectual approach despite - though also *because of* - her own status as a Wiccan. Adler, whose career in journalism saw her work as an NPR correspondent for 35 years, positioned herself as the ideal public voice for a Neopagan movement which championed progressive values, ecological activism, polytheism, education and women's leadership, whilst disavowing what she viewed as the authoritarianism and dogma rife within monotheistic religions.

Born in 1946 in Little Rock, Arkansas, Adler's parentage seems appropriate for a woman who would grow first into a political revolutionary, then a spiritual one too. Her father - a son of Sigmund Freud's eminent contemporary Alfred Adler - worked as a psychiatrist, whilst her politically active but depressive and unpredictable mother had been a staple on the bohemian scene of 1930s Greenwich Village. Raised in Manhattan, socially-anxious Adler described feeling eclipsed by both her mother's physical beauty and her captivating, extroverted presence. She escaped into the world of Greek mythology, inspired by lessons at New York's City and Country School. These imaginative forays would later prove foundational to her faith. She writes in *Drawing Down the Moon*:

> *'The fantasies enabled me to contact stronger parts of myself, to embolden my vision of myself. Besides, these experiences were filled with power, intensity, and even ecstasy that, on reflection, seemed religious or spiritual.'*

Shelving these ecstatic experiences as childhood fancies, Adler went on to study political science at that West Coast hotbed of 1960s civil disobedience - the University of California at Berkeley. She became highly active in the Free Speech Movement's enduring political protest, worked to register African American voters in Mississippi, and embraced what she called "the ecstasy of politics", even when that meant being arrested and jailed for her strident beliefs. Upon graduation she pursued a career in journalism, returning eastwards to complete a Master's Degree at Columbia University. She retained a firm grip on her involvement with activism however, taking part in the Cuban sugar harvest with the Venceremos Brigade, a student organisation founded in 1969 in solidarity with Cuba's struggles against US government policies such as the ongoing economic blockade.

Adler's career in journalism never faltered, with output remaining steady throughout the years of her life. In 1972 she created, produced and hosted the radio show *Hour of the Wolf* for WBAI-FM. Named after the Ingmar Bergman horror film of the same name, the show - which focuses on speculative fiction and has seen many of sci-fi and fantasy's big hitters interviewed - still airs today. During this period Adler's politics took a turn towards the environmental, as she began a search for what she termed an "ecological religious framework". In this endeavour she was particularly inspired by the work of two historians - Arnold Toynbee and Lynn White, who wrote of the overarching anthropocentrism at the heart of Christianity and endemic to Western responses to the ecological crisis. Reading nature writers such as Rachel Carson, Adler rekindled those ecstatic experiences she'd had as a child, re-enchanting her worldview and exploding her politics from a person-centred set of ideas to a wider politics of the planet.

During these explorations of Earth-based practices, Adler received word from a coven in Essex, England, led by Doris and Vic Stewart, who sold taped rituals for $15 each. As Adler couldn't afford these she mentioned that she had a radio show and would like a sample copy. Though she joked with friends about how outlandishly comical corresponding with witches was, the taped ritual changed her perspective entirely; in a 1990 interview with *FireHeart* magazine, she recalled:

> *'Suddenly, here were these people who were adults who were doing this. They were clearly all right, and they were intelligent... I was extremely moved, and I started crying. And then I started writing to these people. Their letters were like the Rosetta stone.'*

By the time of that vital meeting with a literary agent, Adler was a practising Gardnerian Wiccan, progressing through the tradition's degrees (we shall be hearing more of Gardnerian Wicca's namesake,

Gerald Gardner, in Chapter Two). Once she had secured the book deal for *Drawing Down the Moon*, a vast research project got underway which saw Adler spend six months travelling across the US, scouring the country for practitioners of Neopaganism and learning about their varied experiences and beliefs. She defined Neopaganism as a set of modern, polytheistic, nature-based religions. Through her research she uncovered an expansive array of religious ideas and practices which, despite their diversity, were largely united by their core values of environmentalism, feminism, liberation and personal growth. In particular she focused on the growing number of Wiccan groups and solitary Wiccan practitioners in the US.

With Wicca relatively new to the US, many key figures in the movement posited the religion as having ancient roots in the pre-Christian era, hailing it as 'the Old Religion' which had been driven underground by the witch trials of the Early Modern period, only to resurface thanks to the repeal of Great Britain's 1775 Witchcraft Act in 1951. This 'Witch-Cult' hypothesis had been concocted in the 1800s by the German scholars Karl Ernst Jarcke and Franz Josef Mone, then popularised in the late 19th and early 20th century by folklorist Charles Godfrey Leland and Egyptologist Margaret Murray. Such theories have largely been discredited by mainstream academics, though there is a resurgence in interest on this topic from more leftfield scholars in the present day. Adler had experienced the confusion that this theory wrought first-hand during her time with a Welsh coven which had fractured over the question of whether their tradition dated back to 1939 or to 12,000 years ago.

With deep respect and sensitivity towards her readership, Adler argued in *Drawing Down the Moon* that whilst there was a possibility of some continuous strands of a universal pagan belief system throughout history, not only was this highly debatable, but also that religions such as Wicca *not* having a great deal in common with older, pre-Christian forms of belief and practice need not detract from their relevance to modern life. In this sense, Adler succeeded in bringing her sharp intellect to the Craft from her experiences both inside and outside of its bounds; despite undercutting contemporary attempts to legitimise the predominant narrative of the Old Religion, she absolutely honoured and centred the power of myths and folklore whilst tactfully noting that faux historical narratives were common to the development of many religions.

Drawing Down the Moon argues a strong case for Neopaganism as a vital set of religious beliefs that are well suited to modern times. The book dismisses damaging stereotypes popular even today, such as the (largely) misguided notion that Neopagans shun technology and science. What emerges is a vivid picture of an incredibly diverse set of Earth-centred spiritualities which typically champion the rights of all beings in a way that is compassionate, flexible and self-reflective. Whilst noting the positive emergence of, for example, LGBT spiritual groups, Adler also addressed sticking points in the movement, such as the involvement of Neo-Nazis with streams of Heathenism and Norse-oriented beliefs. As a journalist, she never shied away from controversies and the maintenance of a critical gaze.

The book's publication, together with Adler's public life as a journalist for NPR, inadvertently combined to catapult her into the position of a figurehead and spokesperson for Wicca. Along with possessing an ever-astute political mind, this enabled her to forge positions of leadership both within the Craft and in an interfaith capacity. Adler became an elder in the Covenant of the Goddess, a cross-traditional group of Wiccan practitioners and affiliated covens which fought for Wiccans' legal rights and greater collaboration within the Craft. Further to this was a trustee position with the Parliament of Religions and time spent on the Board of the Covenant of Unitarian Universalist Pagans (CUUPS).

Despite these positions, Adler continued her grassroots work attending festivals, teaching courses and running women's spirituality groups. She valued empowering women to feel at home in their bodies; something she had perhaps uncovered herself both through participation in women's conscious-raising groups in the 1970s, and the Craft's very grounded, body-centred rituals and affirmations. A growing into the light, of sorts, from the shadow cast by her mother's beauty and strong presence all those years ago. Perhaps she meant something like this when she described her mother's death, from lung cancer in 1970, as a "liberation". Championing Pagan polytheism as an alternative to the possibilities for patriarchal authoritarianism inherent in monotheistic religions, Adler taught the multiple nature of the Goddess at the heart of Wicca, reminding students of Goddess-worshipping's connections to indigenous cultures across the world. As ever, her spiritual views, though drawn from a well deep inside herself, expanded outwards across the planet at large.

Adler's 1988 handfasting with her long-term partner John Gliedman, an experimental psychologist and science writer, was the first handfasting to feature in the *New York Times* - a landmark moment for Wiccans across the world. When John was diagnosed with terminal stomach cancer, Adler's obsession with the undead began. Reading over 260 books about vampires in swift succession, she eventually wrote two of her own - *Out for Blood* (2013) and *Vampires are Us: Understanding Our Love Affair with the Immortal Dark Side* (2014). Whilst Adler's interests in the topic had been inspired by questions of mortality clearly pertinent to her during John's illness, she uncovered a theme at the heart of vampire-related pop culture which was much bigger than desires for longevity - the theme of political power. Adler outlined her thoughts on vampires at the Second International Convocation of Unitarian Universalist Women held in Romania in 2012, noting the correspondences between late 19th century and early 21st century pop cultural fixations on vampires. She suggested that the connection between these two eras was a similar, unconscious response to increasing globalisation and the brutal acts of colonisation which the West had committed: firstly with the colonisation of indigenous people and their land, then latterly with the colonisation of the planet's key natural resource - oil. In a way, Adler would go on to write, each era creates a bloodsucker for its own time, so that we might reflect the cruelties of the age back to ourselves.

Despite reporting on many of her lifetime's key political events such as 9/11, and writing about heavily divisive topics such as religion, power and money, Adler kept a sense of humour and warmth entangled with the seriousness of her subjects. In *Out for Blood* she admits that during her peak vampire obsession she "walked into a hair salon with a picture of Alice Cullen from the first *Twilight* movie and said "I would like something pixie-ish like that"." She embraced a lightness, an impishness, a dry wit that refreshingly countered the often highly cultivated, grave dispositions and sensibilities of the male forefathers in the occult world who we shall encounter throughout this book.

Adler was diagnosed with endometrial cancer in 2011, the year after John had died. She loved to walk for miles around her beloved New York City, even as her health grew increasingly poor. In the summer of 2014 she passed away aged 68. On Halloween that year, close friends and family gathered to celebrate her life with a private memorial service held at All Souls Unitarian Universalist Church, New York. At the service, Adler's contemporary Starhawk, herself a very public ecofeminist Pagan, quoted a passage from *Vampires are Us*:

> 'We are all part of the life cycle. Like a seed we are born, we sprout, we grow, we mature and decay, making room for future generations who, like seedlings, are reborn through us. As for the persistence of consciousness, deep down, I thought, 'How can we know?"

Photo of Wiccan Priestess Doreen Valiente.
Courtesy of The Doreen Valiente Foundation.

Chapter Two

Doreen Valiente
Mother of Modern Witchcraft
(d. 1999)

In October 1964, fifteen years before Margot Adler published *Drawing Down the Moon*, around fifty witches from across England gathered at a dinner held by the newly-formed Witchcraft Research Association. Although its life span would prove short, the Association aimed to address the controversies surrounding the 'Witch-Cult' hypothesis, and to serve as a unifying force in the increasingly fractious and factional world of Wicca. The organisation's president at this time - Doreen Valiente - hoped that the Association might eventually become the "United Nations of the Craft":

> *'What we need now, more than anything, is for people of spiritual vision to combine together... if only people in the occult world devoted as much time and energy to positive constructive work as they do to denouncing and denigrating each other, their spiritual contribution to the world would be enormous!'*

This speech, in all of its rousing clarity, summarised so much of Valiente's approach to witchcraft and magic. Often lauded as the "mother of modern witchcraft", Valiente's attitude was one of inclusivity, but also discernment. As a prolific writer of books, poetry and Wiccan liturgy, she ensured her words and offerings were accessible to all. Behind her warm tone of guidance there was a sharp, shrewd researcher and fierce believer in authenticity, integrity, and social justice.

Born in Surrey, 1922, to parents who were, in her own words, "brought up Chapel", Valiente would later laugh off claims that she was in fact the illegitimate child of the Great Beast, occultist and founder of the Thelemite religion - Aleister Crowley. Whilst the reality - being the daughter of a land surveyor and architect - might seem less interesting, young Valiente's experiences were far from ordinary. As an adult, she reminisced about her mystical experiences and encounters with the uncanny as a child, and according to her biographer Philip Heselton, she was making poppets and had grown into an accomplished herbalist by her teens.

Valiente's work during the Second World War is thought to have been of a sensitive nature, as she was most likely based at Bletchley Park - the code-breaking centre of the Allied Forces. After a brief marriage which ended in her husband's loss at sea, she moved to Bournemouth with her second husband, Casimiro Valiente. It is on that stretch of England's southern coast that her interest in the occult spiralled. Trawling local public libraries for esoteric texts, Valiente began her studies in earnest; from Spiritualism to Theosophy, she gobbled up everything she could lay her hands on. Never one to forgo the practical aspects of learning, Valiente attended a Spiritualist church (at which she read aloud a Crowley text she had discovered), as well as joining a local parlour group that discussed esoteric matters. Around this time she also began practising ceremonial magic with an artist friend who went by the magical name "Zerki", and together they would work rituals in his flat which were influenced by the Hermetic Order of the Golden Dawn. Valiente chose her own, John Dee-inspired magical name at this time too - she would go by "Ameth", meaning "truth".

After years of intensive magical study and research, Valiente entered into a correspondence that would lay the foundations for her later renown as a witch. A lifelong collector of newspaper articles about occult matters of all sorts, in 1952 she came across a piece in *Illustrated* magazine titled *Witchcraft in Britain*, which mentioned a coven of British witches who had performed a ritual in the New Forest during 1940, attempting to prevent Hitler from invading Britain. In 1951 the last vestiges of the Witchcraft Act, outlawing such occult actions, had been repealed, and Gerald Gardner - who we briefly met in Chapter One, and who happened to be the "resident witch" of a museum of magic on the Isle of Man - had started courting media coverage, including via the article discovered by Valiente. In her book *The Rebirth of Witchcraft* (1989), she recalls feeling incredibly excited by Gardner's references to witchcraft as being "fun", which seemed a very novel idea at the time. Writing to the museum's founder, Cecil Williamson, Valiente's letter was answered by Gardner, and their correspondence began. Gardner had been initiated into the New Forest coven by a witch known as "Dafo", and it was at Dafo's house that Valiente met with him for the first time. She describes this significant event in one of her books:

> 'We seemed to take an immediate liking to each other... One felt that he had seen for horizons and encountered strange things; and yet there was a sense of humour about him, and a youthfulness, in spite of his silver hair.'

Valiente was initiated into Gardner's Bricket Wood coven a year later (without the knowledge of her husband, who remained a sceptic). Notably, hinting at the import she gave to magical provenance, Valiente recognised that many of Gardner's words and actions at her initiation bore a resemblance to those of Crowley and the folklorist Charles Godfrey Leland. Over time, Valiente grew increasingly suspicious with regards to Gardner's "ancient" sources and criticised his overuse of Crowley's texts. Eventually, according to Valiente, Gardner's response to her criticisms was along the lines of "if you think you can do better, get on with it!" Never one to shy away from a challenge, she did, and went on to rewrite many of Gardner's rituals to great effect. Indeed, Professor Ronald Hutton notes that Valiente's words for the *White Moon Charge* "gave Wicca a theology as well as its finest piece of liturgy".

Gardner's hunger for publicity grew over the course of the pair's time together, and with increasing press coverage came more coven members, but also greater media sensationalism and public ire. Valiente, by now the coven's High Priestess, disapproved - preferring Wicca to make itself known through its books rather than being filtered through the lenses of journalists keen for a throwaway headline. And so, Valiente broke with Gardner's coven, founding a new one with her allies which would practice Gardnerian Wicca without being beholden to its namesake or its laws (which she believed had no provenance more ancient than Gardner's imagination). She also believed that there was work to be done in terms of finding the real 'Old Religion'; the pre-Christian Pagan rites that promised to be more authentic than Gardner's patchwork versions. Indeed, long after many Wiccans had accepted the dismantling of theories regarding the 'Old Religion', Valiente continued to grant the Craft the possibility of an ancient provenance, remaining largely loyal to the visions of both Margaret Murray and Charles Godfrey Leland.

During her lifetime, along with publishing numerous books, Valiente was initiated into four covens in total. There was a pattern to her dances with covens - that of becoming involved, doubting provenance and patriarchal coven leadership, doing research to confirm any suspicions, then moving on. Her political alliances followed a similar structure, including a brief foray into right-wing politics during the early 1970s. Heselton suggests that during her 18-month stint with the National Front she might have in fact been undercover and spying for the state. She herself claimed disillusionment as the reason for her separation from the Front. A firm believer in women's rights, gay rights, and civil liberties, we might wonder why she joined such an organisation at all, if not to uncover insider information about the enemy.

In *The Rebirth of Witchcraft* Valiente was explicit about her feminism, and her distaste for so many covens, stating that "we were allowed to call ourselves High Priestesses, Witch Queens and similar fancy titles; but we were still in the position of having men running things". Like Adler, Valiente valued collaboration over domination, and held out hopes for a "constructive" spirituality that emphasised the environment, civil liberties and social justice rather than petty squabbles and battles over authority. More than this, she wanted to promote a witchcraft that was open to all. LGBTQ+ folks were part of this equitable vision for the Craft too, with Valiente noting, "What right have we to insist that people who were born with feelings different from ours shall be debarred from worshipping the most ancient powers of life?" This flowed from her now canonical version of *The Charge of the Goddess*, which explicitly states that "all acts of love and pleasure are my rituals" (most likely adapted from Crowley's *Liber DCCCXXXVII - The Law of Liberty*, which reads, "remember that all acts of love and pleasure are rituals, must be rituals").

In this sense, as well as believing - or at least hoping - that Wicca's roots extended far back into the distant past, Valiente repeatedly celebrated the religion's possibilities for moving forwards. In her 1997 address to the National Conference of the Pagan Federation, she stated:

> *'We have literally spread worldwide. We are a creative and fertile movement. We have inspired art, literature, television, music and historical research. We have lived down the calumny and abuse. We have survived treachery. So it seems to me that the 'Powers That Be' must have a purpose for us in the Aquarian Age that is coming into being.'*

Valiente spoke often of the Aquarian Age - an astrological time period which she and countless others maintained would herald a new dawn of liberation, environmental consciousness and freedom from patriarchal constraints. For her, the surge of interest in occult matters and practices was all part of this grand and thrilling future. Her exuberant enthusiasm for the Craft's expansion and forward momentum - which she herself was in no small part responsible for - begs the question as to whether Gardner could have created Wicca as we know it without the assistance of her natural leadership capabilities, sense of hope, and flair for liturgical writing.

Despite her ever-increasing celebrity, Valiente remained incredibly down to earth. An enthusiastic football fan, she enjoyed betting on horses and throughout her life worked in a surprising array of jobs - including stints in factories, for a furniture company, and in the Brighton branch of Boots pharmacy. Following the death of Casimiro, she never remarried but spent her remaining 20 years with the "love of her life", Ron Cooke, who she initiated into the Craft, with him becoming her High Priest. And so, the pair's life came to revolve around holidays in Glastonbury, football matches on the TV, Valiente's writing and public engagements, and the practice and study of magic.

Valiente died in 1999, two years after Ron had passed away, and her ashes were scattered around the roots of her favourite oak tree near the South Downs in East Sussex. Two of those present picked an acorn from the tree, cast it in silver, and gifted acorn pendants to those at the Museum of Witchcraft and Magic in Boscastle, Cornwall. This museum, founded by Cecil Williamson, was the successor to Williamson's earlier iteration on the Isle of Man which Valiente had read about in 1952, and which had played such a vital role in her early life as a Wiccan. A perfectly full circle narrative for an avidly full circle witch.

Marjorie Cameron as the Scarlet Woman from Kenneth Anger's 1954 movie *The Inauguration of the Pleasure Dome*, Photographed by Kenneth Anger.

Chapter Three

Marjorie Cameron
Muse No More
(d. 1995)

In the mid-1950s, the American artist and occultist Marjorie Cameron Parsons Kimmel met experimental filmmaker Kenneth Anger. One of the United States' first openly gay filmmakers, Anger's work melds hallucinogenic psychodrama with occult themes drawn largely from his experiences and beliefs as a follower of Thelema, the religious movement Aleister Crowley founded in 1904. Anger was the perfect collaborator for Cameron, whose paintings and drawings incorporated her own relationship with Thelema, unconscious dream-states, and autobiography. At this first meeting, Cameron declared "I am the Scarlet Woman", referencing the title Crowley gave to his magical partners. Anger replied, "I've been waiting to meet you for a thousand years". Declaring herself the sole bearer of this grand mantle might seem to be an act of egotism on Cameron's part, but tracing the story of her life we discover that there is even more complexity to her claim than might first appear.

Cameron would go on to replace iconic French writer Anaïs Nin as the Scarlet Woman in Anger's 38-minute masterpiece of ritual film, *Inauguration of the Pleasure Dome* (1954). Inspired by the aesthetic innovation of avant-garde luminaries such as Maya Deren (we will meet her in Chapter 8), Anger's film elevates Cameron to the status of occult goddess. Indeed, in many of Crowley's writings the Scarlet Woman appears as an earthly avatar of the Thelemic goddess Babalon, a deity inspired by the following passage in the Bible's *Book of Revelation*:

MUSES NO MORE: PORTRAITS OF OCCULT WOMEN

> *'I saw a woman sit upon a scarlet coloured beast, full of names of blasphemy, having seven heads and ten horns. And the woman was arrayed in purple and scarlet colour, and decked with gold and precious stones and pearls, having a golden cup in her hand full of abominations and filthiness of her fornication: And upon her forehead was a name written, MYSTERY, BABYLON THE GREAT, THE MOTHER OF HARLOTS AND ABOMINATIONS OF THE EARTH.'*

The story of Cameron and her complicated association with Babalon is darkly entwined with that of Crowley and his famed adherent - the rocket scientist and occultist John ("Jack") Whiteside Parsons. Histories of itinerant, elusive Cameron have often sidelined her fullness in favour of these two male heavyweights of the occult sphere. However, her work (both magical and artistic) has received increasing interest in recent years for its fiercely visionary nature and in the latter case, its beguiling linework and surrealist sensibility.

Hailing from a small railroad town in Iowa, Cameron was born in 1922 - the same year that saw Doreen Valiente enter the world. Growing up in a middle class family, Cameron was relatively buffered from the effects of the Great Depression which followed the US stock market collapse of 1929. Nevertheless she faced hardships; tales of sexual engagement with older men abound and according to Spencer Kansa, author of the Cameron biography *Wormwood Star* (2010), she fell pregnant at 15, prompting her mother to perform a home abortion. Talented in the arts, young Cameron took up a job as a department store display artist during World War II, before enlisting in the WAVES (Women Accepted for Volunteer Emergency Services). Admittance to this non-combative arm of the navy saw Cameron employed in Washington as a cartographer, then later as a makeup artist and wardrobe mistress on propaganda films. Despite being court martialed for desertion after going AWOL to visit her injured brother,

Cameron received an honourable discharge in 1945 and returned to her family, who now lived in Pasadena, northeast of downtown Los Angeles.

Pasadena was also home to the maverick rocket scientist Jack Parsons, co-founder of the pioneering Jet Propulsion Laboratory which still operates at the cutting edge of the American space programme today. By night Parsons was a dedicated member of the Ordo Templi Orientis (O.T.O.), an occult organisation with Crowley at its head and Thelema as its heart. Parsons corresponded regularly with Crowley whilst house-sharing with a coterie of fellow O.T.O. associates engaged in polyamory and mysticism long before these practices would swing out from under the radar.

Parsons was ambitious in all areas of his life, writing in a letter to his first wife Helen, "with Thelema as my goal, and the stars as my destination and my home, I have set my eyes on high". After Parsons' girlfriend Betty turned her affections towards one of the house's other residents - L. Ron Hubbard, founder of the Church of Scientology - the intensity of his magical practices escalated. Writing to Crowley, he explained, "I need a magical partner. I have many experiments in mind. I hope my elemental gets off the dime". Commencing in January 1946, Parsons performed a series of daily invocations (involving solo magical masturbation) to bring his "elemental" into being. Together with his love-rival Hubbard, he drove out to the Mojave Desert, where Parsons intuited that the magical operation was complete. Arriving home, he found 23 year old Cameron on his doorstep, paying a visit to this house of magic and free love on the invitation of a naval friend. The first segment of the Babalon Working was complete.

The two became instant lovers, spending a fortnight shut away in Parson's room together. "I have my elemental!" a thrilled Parsons wrote to Crowley. Of their two weeks in bed, he commented, "I am to invoke continually, this now being possible and easy". For Parsons, this period was apparently filled with frenzied sex magic, though Cameron recalled that she "didn't know very much [about] Jack's magical work. In fact, I probably derided it." These differing accounts ask us to consider the issue of consent in magical practice - how much did Jack tell her about the work he was engaged in during those two weeks? Contemporary social and legal ethics acknowledge that sex acts require consent, but whether the occult world grapples effectively with this in relation to acts of sex magic is debatable.

In possession of his magical partner, Parsons now desired to manifest the goddess Babalon in human form, ushering in a new age of Dionysian sexual, social and political freedom. In *The Eloquent Blood: The Goddess Babalon and the Construction of Femininities in Western Esotericism* (2020), Dr. Manon Hedenborg White explains that, "Parsons construed Babalon as a bloodthirsty revolutionary, a living messiah, the quintessential new aeon woman, and the goddess of witchcraft". For all of this Cameron was to be the vehicle, and Hubbard would be along for the ride.

Alone in the desert, Parsons divinely received instructions for the next stage of the Babalon Working. Ritual instructions were simultaneously loose and specific:

> 'Make a box of blackness at ten o'clock. Smear the vessel which contains flame with thine own blood. Destroy at the altar a thing of value. Remain in perfect silence, and heed the voice of Our Lady. Speak not of this ritual or of Her coming to any person. If asked, answer in a manner that avoids suspicion. Nor speculate at any time as to Her future mortal identity. To receive flatter-ing communications to thy damnation. Press not to receive teach-ings beyond those given.'

Parsons, in his invocations of Babalon, demonstrated a feminism uncommon for men of his time. It might be said that the new aeon he hoped she would bring about was akin to Valiente and Adler's hopes for women's liberation and a nature based religion. Nevertheless, in their relationship Cameron seems to have been both exalted and objectified by his belief in her status as a magical entity. During this period, Parsons offered sceptical Cameron a crash-course in occult practice, though she would only come to understand the full intricacies and intent of the Babalon Working many years later. Peter Grey writes in *The Two Antichrists* (2021):

> *'Cameron played no part in these formal ritual workings, and was deliberately kept in the dark by Parsons, not in order to leverage a power dynamic, but so that she could demonstrate the unequivocal signs without being prompted, and declare herself Soteira. It was a task she would struggle with the rest of her life.'*

After their marriage in 1946, Cameron traveled alone throughout Europe and Mexico, settling for a time in San Miguel de Allende where she met the surrealist artist Leonora Carrington and indulged her bisexuality with various lovers. When Parsons rocketry career was cut short due to F.B.I. investigations into his occult activities, the couple planned to travel together to Mexico. The day before their departure, Parsons was in his garage laboratory. Dropping a coffee can filled with fulminate of mercury, the resulting explosion ended his life abruptly at the age of 37. His mother, upon hearing the news, took a Nembutal overdose, dying just a handful of hours after her son.

The press gorged on this morbid tragedy bursting with rocket science and "black magic". Cameron fled to the Californian desert, where she lived alone in an abandoned canyon without electricity or running water, turning inwards upon herself and attempting to contact Parsons' spirit. For the rest of her life she would grapple with the question of whether or not she was human, an avatar of Babalon, or Babalon herself. Her mental health, understandably, oscillated. Though her interest in the occult had waxed and waned during her time with Parsons, she committed herself fully now, coming to comprehend the Babalon Working via Parson's remaining papers. With the 1960s around the corner - the decade of sexual revolution, women's increased freedom and ecological consciousness - we might wonder whether the Babalon Working had in fact been successful.

Cameron eventually returned to society. Along with a brief second marriage to a veteran struggling with Post Traumatic Stress Disorder, she gave birth to a daughter, the father unknown. Cameron parented Crystal with a loose leash, continuing to travel restlessly whilst also experimenting heavily with drugs. Her drawing *Peyote Vision*, created during a psychedelic trip, featured in a show at Ferus Gallery in 1957. Depicting a serpent-tongued woman having sex with an alien being, the work led to the exhibition being shut down by the L.A. Vice Squad. The gallerist was arrested whilst Cameron was charged with obscenity. According to Scott Hobbs (director of the Cameron Parsons Foundation), "she vowed never to show her work after the ruckus at Ferus". Coupled with this, Cameron ritualistically burned many of her artworks, as if to separate herself from the spiritual emissions contained within them. This included nearly all of the paintings featured in *The Wormwood Star* (1956), Curtis Harrington's 10 minute film portrait of Cameron.

Despite working outside of the gallery system, Cameron's work was as prolific as her varied social life on the underground art scene, and seems to have drawn from a deep well of personal mythos, self exploration and cosmic reckoning. In her later years, Cameron devoted a great deal of time to her grandchildren and the practice of Tai chi. She painted, smoked pot and offered friendship to younger occultists such as William Breeze, the O.T.O.'s current international leader. She died of cancer aged 73, with a photograph of Parsons by her hospital bedside. The O.T.O.'s Soror Helena administered the Thelemic last rites.

It has taken many years for Cameron's art to receive recognition, and much is owed to the Cameron Parsons Foundation for highlighting her work and introducing it to a wider audience, both together with - and independent of - Parson's oeuvre of writings. Cameron's surviving paintings and drawings can be viewed as documents of her magical workings and preoccupations. Movement and velocity thread throughout them, reflecting her itinerant, restless lifestyle and the transformations birthed within her as a result of both her occult practices and repeated changes in environment. The majority of Cameron's work is figurative - there are elements of portraiture at play but she also brings to life chimerical entities through scrawling lines lashed out like exorcisms. Perhaps they were. Engagement with male sexuality is evident too. In a drawing which illustrates Parsons' poem *Punch* we see a male figure with an erect phallus, framing a woman as she falls through space. Works such as these suggest that, contrary to Grey's thesis, Cameron was highly aware of power dynamics at play in her relationship with Parsons. In fact, it seems like something she is not only working through, but also seeking to subvert by asserting her agency. We see this depicted in the women she draws, often with flame-like shapes exuding from their genitalia.

Posthumously, Cameron's identity as more than a muse has come to the fore. Almost a decade after Cameron's death a surge of attention was directed towards her life and work. Fulgur Press released *Songs for the Witch Woman* (2014) - a facsimile edition of Parson's evocative, obsessive poetry and Cameron's inky, formidable art. Robert Garrova, writing in the *Los Angeles Review of Books* notes that the work reads like "a call and response between two lovers". In many ways, it is. The final part of the book reveals Cameron's activities in the aftermath of Parsons' death; diary entries document a magical working in the desert which sees her attempting to contact her Holy Guardian Angel, as described by Crowley in his book *Magick Without Tears* (1954). Given Cameron's deep state of grief, it is unsurprising that she should want to conjure a guiding force which might assist her in conducting life beyond Parsons. Yet at times it remains unclear in this diary whether she is calling to her Guardian Angel or, in fact, her lost husband:

> *'Oh ruthless lover I have forgotten thy name is love and I know you not as thou promised. And I shall come again with the food for thy indifferent gut - and thou shalt leave me only thy derisive laughing. And even this is thy fearful blessing.'*

How confusing, to be in the very human state of mourning whilst also grappling with uncertainty as to whether or not one is even human at all. Through carrying on Parsons' magical work we can only assume that Cameron was able to hold tightly to the memory (or spirit) of the man she loved. Yet the chaotic, fractured way in which her life unfolded - Kansa suggests she may have been institutionalised at least once - reveals just how vulnerable she was both following Parsons death *and* her somewhat problematic 'involvement' in his magical workings. Rather than considering whether the story of her life reflects madness or magic, we might notice how thin the veil dividing the two is.

Sybil Leek, *Witch at Craft in Burley* - 19 October 1963

Chapter Four

Sybil Leek
Witch Next Door
(d. 1982)

Let us head back over the pond to 1960s England, home of the newly formed Witchcraft Research Association (WRA). Although Doreen Valiente presided over the organisation at the time of its first meeting, its founder was a rather eccentric acquaintance of hers. Sybil Leek - by her publisher's proclamation "the most famous witch of the century" - was an ardent believer in the 'Witch-Cult' hypothesis and created the WRA partly to prove it, in addition to uniting witches across Britain under a shared banner. According to Ronald Hutton, Leek's formation of the WRA was inspired by both the recent death of Gerald Gardner and the rousing lecture tour of Russell Hope Robbins, an academic and author of *The Encyclopedia of Witchcraft and Demonology* (1959). Robbins' lecture tour held the undermining of Margaret Murray's thesis at its heart. Hutton writes:

> 'She attended his address to the Folk-Lore Society, equipped with her pet jackdaw (or 'familiar') Hotfoot Jackson, who sat upon her shoulder and was encouraged to croak loudly whenever Robbins said something of which she disapproved.'

Leek was not in attendance at the WRA's inaugural dinner. In fact, Valiente had succeeded Leek after the latter was forced to resign; fleeing Britain for sanctuary in America. As we shall go on to discover, Leek's fame had rapidly soured into infamy on her home turf - a very modern day witch hunt fuelled by television cameras and sensationalist newspaper headlines.

Sybil Leek was born in 1917 in Staffordshire, England. According to her autobiography *Diary of a Witch* (1968) she came into this world at a crossroads where three rivers meet, and was in possession of a "witch-mark", a sign which during the peak of the 17th century witch trials would have condemned her as being touched by the Devil himself. Leek stated that she could claim the longest lineage in witch history, and that she had traced ancestors back to 1134 AD. By her own account she had an idyllic and mystical childhood, recalling the way her grandmother drew astrological symbols on pastries, whilst she learned plant identification from her aunt and discussed Eastern philosophies with her father. Following three years of formal schooling - during which she reportedly got into trouble for astral projecting into another classroom - she took up a job as a local news reporter whilst receiving tuition in magic from her grandmother. For Leek, "occultism simply seeks knowledge beyond the range of ordinary perceptions". As the author of over 20 books, occult knowledge would become a lifelong currency for her, but at quite a price.

Despite being warmly engaged with family life, Leek eloped with a concert pianist in her late teens. Following her husband's death a few years later, she was initiated into a coven in France, of which the High Priestess was "a distant Russian aunt". Upon returning to England, she befriended the Roma of the New Forest, eventually living with them for almost a year and communicating with her family via telepathy whenever they required her presence. During this period, as well as learning midwifery and solidifying her knowledge of herbs, Leek was an active member of the Horsa Coven which met regularly outside the nearby village of Burley.

Leek's next adventure saw her open two antique shops - one in Somerset and one in the New Forest, for which she claimed to have acquired goods using Extra Sensory Perception. Around this time she also became a reporter for Southern TV. Leek continued to juggle these responsibilities following her promotion to the position of High Priestess of the Horsa Coven shortly before the repeal of the

Witchcraft Act in 1951. Of this landmark occasion Leek writes in *Diary of a Witch*:

> 'The world even now is not yet ready for witchcraft, as I know all too well. But then I was wildly enthusiastic, young enough to believe that the injustice of centuries could be wiped out in a few years.'

It was perhaps this enthusiasm which led her to "confess" to the press; on 16th September 1963 the *Daily Herald* published the headline *YES I AM THE FOREST WITCH*, along with a photo of Leek in the antique shop with her ever present jackdaw, Hotfoot Jackson (named for his warm claws, which Valiente attested to). A media frenzy ensued, with her fellow villagers divided over the presence of a celebrity witch in their midst. Leek's landlord was very much not on side, ousting her and her family from their home and refusing to renew the lease on the shop. The fires of outrage were further stoked by the ritual vandalism of churches that winter - five in Sussex and one near Leek's home. At Bamber Church in Sussex, magical symbols were scrawled across the building's door in chalk. Leek visited the site, either in her capacity as reporter or as an interested occult researcher, and translated what she recognised as the Theban alphabet: "We dedicate this church to our Lady of the Jackdaw". In *The Rebirth of Witchcraft* (1989), Valiente writes,

> '[Leek] had a suspicion as to the identity of the leading practitioner of black magic who was responsible for these outrages. She had taxed him with it when he called to see her at her home in the New Forest. He wanted her help as a healer to cure him of an illness from which he was suffering. In return, she required from him a promise that he would never bring his evil practice to the New Forest again.'

The ever increasing scandal surrounding Leek forced her to resign from the recently founded WRA and saw her flee to the US with her husband and two sons. There she completed a highly successful lecture tour, published countless books and became a darling of radio and television talk shows, much to her purse's delight. In *My Life in Astrology* (1972), she notes the benefits of her jet setting lifestyle:

> *'It behooves the traveling author to develop a certain technique for traveling. Even so, there are many times when she wonders if it is worthwhile, but the consolation comes when the royalties begin to arrive. Didn't I say the name of the game was money?'*

Whilst many people throughout her career would proclaim her a fame-hungry charlatan, Leek is refreshingly open about the driving forces behind her career choices - her hopes for a more inclusive, witch-welcoming world, and also the fact that she simply "needed work". An astute businesswoman with an eye for the prize and the savvy of a media professional, Sybil Leek Incorporated was founded in 1964. In Leek's case, we might use the term *shameless* in its most glorious, liberated and fabulous light. She was a working woman, earning her living at a time when many mothers continued to live domestic lives with little option or opportunity for much else. Like Margot Adler's Wicca, Leek believed that her Old Religion was feminist at its core, writing proudly that "Witchcraft is the only religion which enables a woman to take a major part in it when initiated, to retain her feminine identity and be a complete human being, not a second-class member of a religious fraternity."

There is something awe-inspiring about Leek's capacity to keep on talking; to keep on raising awareness of witchcraft via her many television and radio talk show appearances in the US, in spite of - or perhaps because of - her grim history of maltreatment in the UK. Hounded as both a madwoman and fraud, she continued to speak out, arguing the case for acceptance of otherness with both eloquence and thoughtfulness. As with her contemporary Valiente, Leek made witchcraft seem appealing and accessible by deeming the common trappings of occult language or obscure references unnecessary. Here was a set of practices and beliefs to be taken seriously, thrown into the limelight following the repeal of the Witchcraft Act. To argue the case for magic's freedom in this new era was to be political, defiant, courageous. Leek was all of these, turning her trial by media into an impressive victory.

After a stint in New York, Leek made homes in Houston and Las Vegas, where she formed a new kind of Wicca with Charmaine Dey and Tarostar called Sacred Pentagraph. This emerging tradition followed an occult lodge system and focused its attention on the cyclical Wiccan calendar of the year with its associated rituals. The three founding witches initially referred to themselves as the Ancient Order of the Bell, Book and Candle, a phrase which pays homage to a method of excommunication (by 'anathema', or ritual shunning) from the Roman Catholic Church which had been introduced by Pope Zachary in the 8th century. A fitting and typically witty mantle for someone who had been shunned by both the public and her peers, only to be deemed sideshow entertainment for the media's gawkers (though this relationship certainly offered mutual rewards).

Sybil Leek settled in Florida for the final fifteen years of her life. She died of cancer aged 65. Her ashes were taken back to the UK for burial and - demonstrating her celebrity - an obituary was published in the *New York Times*. Though Leek's books are currently out of print, covens in the Sacred Pentagraph tradition continue to operate today, proud to be connected to her (somewhat outrageously) long lineage of witches.

Madeline Montalban (n.d.)

Chapter Five

Madeline Montalban
Lady of Lucifer
(d. 1982)

𝕳ere's how the story goes: in the mid-1920s, sixteen year old Madeline Montalban - a difficult, capricious child - was packed off to London by her father with a large cheque in hand. Arriving on Aleister Crowley's doorstep at Half Moon Street she was greeted by one of his Scarlet Women and told that Crowley was upstairs in the bath having an asthma attack. Well versed in such situations, the young Madeline proffered medication from her handbag and all was well. Crowley was so grateful for Madeline's assistance that he took his entourage out to The Savoy for dinner that night, her father's cheque in his pocket.

Whether such a tale is true or not - it brings to mind Marjorie Cameron's legendary arrival on Jack Parsons' doorstep - we shall never know for sure. According to her student Michael Howard (editor of *The Cauldron* magazine), Montalban actually met Crowley for the first time in the 1930s, at the age of 23, having been sent to interview him for the *Daily Express*. A friendship blossomed, and she spoke of acting as a seer in some of his Thelemic rituals. Montalban's opinion of Crowley as a magician was not a particularly high one, however. She told Howard that Crowley "was not a true magician because he could not master astrology properly". And with that, she put the 'Great Beast' in his place.

Much of the information to be gleaned about this vital figure in British Luciferianism and magic survives through word-of-mouth, particularly via the wonderfully rich anecdotes collected in Julia Phillips' biographical volume *Madeline Montalban: The Magus of St. Giles* (2012). Whilst several of the occult women we have met so far were prolific authors of magical books, Montalban was not. Renowned within certain circles, she was secretive, often used pseudonyms, and kept the bulk of her public writing on occult topics within the realm of magazines such as the popular esoteric publication *Prediction*. This means that the details of Montalban's life are difficult to trace, unjustly diminishing her renown in the present day as a pioneer of Luciferianism, a skilled teacher, and a beloved member of London's bustling mid-century occult scene.

Born in the English seaside town of Blackpool in 1910, Sylvia Madeline Royals would later go by many names - Dolores del Castro, Regina Norcliff, Athene Deluce, Nina de Luna, Lucien Stevens, and of course Madeline Montalban. Bedridden with polio as a child, Montalban turned to the Old Testament for sustenance, uncovering narratives and concepts that would remain central to her life until the grave. Montalban would never declare herself a Christian, though many of her later students arrived at her work having tread that path.

However she ended up in London, Montalban began work as a journalist, writing for publications such as *London Life* from around 1930. Phillips, in tracing Montalban's story, has found no prior connection between London and the Royals family, suggesting that Montalban truly was going it alone; an adventurous quest for a young woman of this era to embark upon. Madeline certainly had a reputation for her formidable presence. Jo Logan, Montalban's editor at *Prediction* between 1976 and 1982, speaks to these qualities in an interview with Julia Phillips: "there was an amazing sense of glamour about her, an energy she possessed that made you see what she wanted you to see, not what was really there". As well as glamour in the more mundane, contemporary sense, we might posit that Montalban was also versed in glamour in the magical sense - the Scots word *gramarye*, later anglicised as *glamour*, refers to a spell cast to alter the shape of reality. This act of glamour*ing* is an illusion and deception carefully designed to assert power over those grasped in its thrall. Ilise S. Carter describes the way in which, for example, a single tool of glamour - the seemingly innocuous lipstick - wields the power to change history. From the Suffragettes to the riot grrrl movement, the act of glamouring others has proven a fierce weapon to wield in the face of misogyny and oppression. It is highly possible that, given anecdotes centering her presence, Montalban utilised such tools and practices. Certainly there seems to have been a changeable, shapeshifting quality to Montalban's personality. Phillips remarks:

> 'Madeline's conflicting drives were expressed through a mercurial personality that was both engaging and frustrating; one moment filled with fun and generosity, the next a darker aspect appeared and those around her ducked for cover. Quite literally in some cases, as Madeline in one of her tempers often caused objects to fly around the room as her incredible psychic energy found its outlet.'

Phillips also describes how the evidence points to Montalban being a self-taught magician, though she certainly surrounded herself with well-known and influential magical peers. Her relationship with Gerald Gardner, for example, was a fascinating one. After the war she was employed by Gardner as a typist for his book *High Magic's Aid* (1949), yet often claimed to have been much more deeply involved in the foundational text's creation. They worked together magically too - in ceremonial magician Kenneth Grant's book *Nightside of Eden* (1977) a ritual is recalled which involved Montalban, Gardner, Grant and his wife Steffi, an unnamed young witch and a sigil designed by occult artist Austin Osman Spare. Despite the proximity of Montalban and Gardner's relationship, Howard tells of how she described Gardner as "a fraud and a pervert" by the mid-1960s. This opinion was purportedly based on a ritual Montalban had attended where she witnessed a young female acolyte tickling Gardner's genitals with a feather whilst he was tied up naked. Such reports regarding Gardner's sexual activities were not uncommon at the time, and these instances are rumoured to have been one of the reasons why Doreen Valiente distanced herself from him during the latter part of his life. Montalban went further than merely distancing herself however - her student Michael Howard was later initiated into Wicca and writes that, "she never forgave me for what she regarded as an act of treachery". What remains unknown is whether Gardner and his acolytes' activities were or were not consensual (though the power differential between the High Priest Gardner and his female disciples is worth considering here). We are left wondering whether Montalban is either prudish - shaming Gardner for his sexual kinks - or aware of sexual misconduct.

In 1946, Montalban made psychic contact with Lucifer for the first time, having worked with this angelic being for two years. She positioned Lucifer (who she called "Lumiel") as a guiding light and teacher of the great mysteries - an instructor and inspiration on the road to enlightenment. Though Christian theology conflates Lucifer with the figure of Satan, this heavenly being significantly predates the religion, with the motif of the fallen angel appearing in the ancient Hebrew apocalyptic text *The Book of Enoch*. A personification of Venus was also venerated in Greco-Roman culture, with Lucifer being the Latin name for the planet in its morning aspect, hence the title "Morning Star". A revivification of this separation between Lucifer and Satan chimed not only with Montalban but with Doreen Valiente too, who comments in *The Rebirth of Witchcraft* (1989) that, "the word Lucifer is simply Latin for 'light-bearer'. Yet it has evidently become confused with the Christian idea of Satan [...] 'The god of the old religion becomes the devil of the new.'" Valiente also refers to Lucifer's appearance in Charles Godfrey Leland's *Aradia, or the Gospel of the Witches* (1899) as the brother/lover of witch queen Diana, the deity at the centre of the Witch-Cult hypothesis.

A decade after her first encounter with Lucifer, Montalban set up an occult correspondence course with Lucifer/Lumiel at the core of its philosophical and practical teachings. This course formed the 'outer court' of the Order of the Morning Star; an esoteric organisation founded by Montalban and her partner Nicholas Heron. In many ways the correspondence course served as a pipeline into the group's deeper and more controversial occult activities concerning Lumiel. Students were not gained through advertisements; they were typically readers of *Prediction* who had written letters to Montalban with a seeker's desire to learn more. Once admitted to the course they were instructed in angelic magic, astrology, tarot, Gnosticism and stellar lore. A central tenet was belief in, and understanding of, the correspondences between the seven planetary bodies of the ancient world and the seven angelic beings that Montalban associated with them. For example, the Sun was associated with Archangel Michael, the Moon with Gabriel, Mars with Samael, Mercury with Raphael, Jupiter with Sachael, Venus with Anael, and Saturn with Cassiel. From these correspondences branched out further webs of correspondence incorporating days, hours, animals, plants and minerals. Intellectual and felt understanding of these lines of power enabled students to construct talismans invoking the presence or qualities of the angel they held in mind.

Like Leek and Valiente, Montalban was highly skilled when it came to making complex topics easily digestible. The matter-of-fact tone adopted in her *Prediction* columns attests to this. Scathing of the complex ceremonial rituals of so many occult orders at the time, Montalban's magical workings were firmly grounded in daily life. She writes in the February 1968 issue of *Prediction* that,

> *'Housewives who find themselves up against a problem that they can't solve [...] should think about it while they clean the windows. Letting extra light into the house can let light into the mind [...] Some rituals are elaborate, especially in magical practice, but I have found that simple "home-made" rituals can be quite as powerful as those needing hours of preparation. The daily*

bath can be as powerful as the long-winded Ritual Bath of the Mages, providing you come out cleansed in both body and mind'.

After completing the first part of the course, dedicated students were invited to partake in more advanced materials. In these closely guarded later lessons the principles of Montalban's flavour of Luciferianism were laid out. Key teachings regarding Lumiel are expounded in the 21 page text *The Book of Lumiel,* which positions Lumiel as a beacon who wishes so greatly for humanity's perfection that he attempts to accelerate their evolution through a "mingling" of angels with "human daughters" (not dissimilar to the more uncouth activities of certain fallen angels in *The Book of Enoch*). These actions lead to chaos and destruction - humanity is not yet advanced enough for enlightenment. As punishment for this experiment, Lucifer is condemned to matter, and now human enlightenment and freedom from matter is dependent upon *his* freedom from matter. In order to teach humans, Lucifer incarnates as, for example, Christ (to the shock of many of Montalban's students). Howard explains that, "If their reaction to this sensational revelation about Lumiel and the Christ was not a negative one, the student might be invited to learn more and enter the OMS [Order of the Morning Star]". Discussing this pivotal lesson, Phillips emphasises the radical nature of these teachings:

> *'She was at the vanguard of those who are only recently coming to understand the important role and purpose of the teaching angels, and in particular, the one known as the* Light Bringer *who is most commonly called* Lucifer. *This lesson is essentially her reinterpretation of the creations of the heavens and earth, the war between the angels, and the importance of the Light Bringer in guiding mankind in its continuing evolution.'*

Montalban's style of teaching followed the Hermetic tradition of using stories and real-life examples to demonstrate points. In light of this, it's certainly worth considering whether her magical "origin" story involving Crowley and his pocketing of her father's cheque was in fact a teaching story, designed to take a dig at ceremonial magic's money-hungry, powerful and patriarchal figures. Nevertheless, Montalban was not above money-spinning herself, and according to Phillips spoke quite plainly about money as a motivating force. To scrabble together a living she not only ran courses (42 in total) but also sold spells for all manner of requirements, and apparently even used her astrological skills to gamble on the Stock Exchange. Montalban was a great believer in effort, hard work and persistence in relation to both material and magical life. In the posthumously compiled *Prediction Book of the Tarot* (1983), she claims the following:

> *'No effort to achieve success is ever wasted. The mental and physical power behind each attempt accumulates on the astral plane; it is placed in our 'occult bank' until the time comes when we have enough power to our credit to overthrow every barrier to our success and our private worlds of happiness can be achieved.'*

We might hope that Montalban's occult bank was overflowing, and that her private world of happiness was joyously full. Although so little of her life has been preserved in the public eye, the Order of the Morning Star continues today, carefully steered by her friends. Further to this, her perspectives and developments in Luciferianism have majorly influenced figures such as her student, Michael Howard, who disseminated and expounded many of her teachings on Lumiel and the Watchers in *Pillars of Tubal Cain* (2000). Her influences are also apparent in the work of the esteemed occultists who went on to found their own traditions, including Alex Sanders (Alexandrian Wicca), Robert Cochrane (The Clan of Tubal Cain) and Andrew D. Chumbley (Cultus Sabbati).

In later life Montalban became an emphatic supporter of the Richard III Society (formerly The Fellowship of the White Boar). The king's reputation over the course of history had been particularly damaged by Shakespeare's antagonistic rendering of the monarch in the play *Richard III*. Montalban's interest in the topic is unsurprising given that Margaret Murray's Witch-Cult hypothesis posited Richard III as the royal leader of the 'Old Religion' in the 15th century. This theory was expanded upon in Murray's book *The Divine King in England* (1954), in which she claims that there is a hidden conspiracy of paganism amongst the nobles of England. There is little doubt that Madeline would have been delighted to live through the discovery, in 2012, of Richard III's skeleton under a carpark in Leicester. Alluringly, Audrey Strange - a member of the Society - had predicted the whereabouts of the lost grave in 1975, but it was Phillipa Langley (the Society's Scottish branch President) who was responsible for the 2012 exhumation. Langley states that, "the first time I stood in that car park, the strangest feeling just washed over me. I thought: 'I am standing on Richard's grave.'" It seems that Montalban wasn't the only member of the Society to have experienced psychic phenomenon.

During the period of Montalban's enthusiasm for the long-dead monarch, she would hold medieval parties where guests consumed wild boar and mead procured from London's most luxurious department store - Harrods. This taste for refinement and celebration carried on until Montalban's death from lung cancer in 1982; her friends told Phillips of how she had champagne brought to the hospital to be shared with staff and her dearest friends. An act of generosity and merrymaking at the darkest of times. A fierce and defiant turn towards the light.

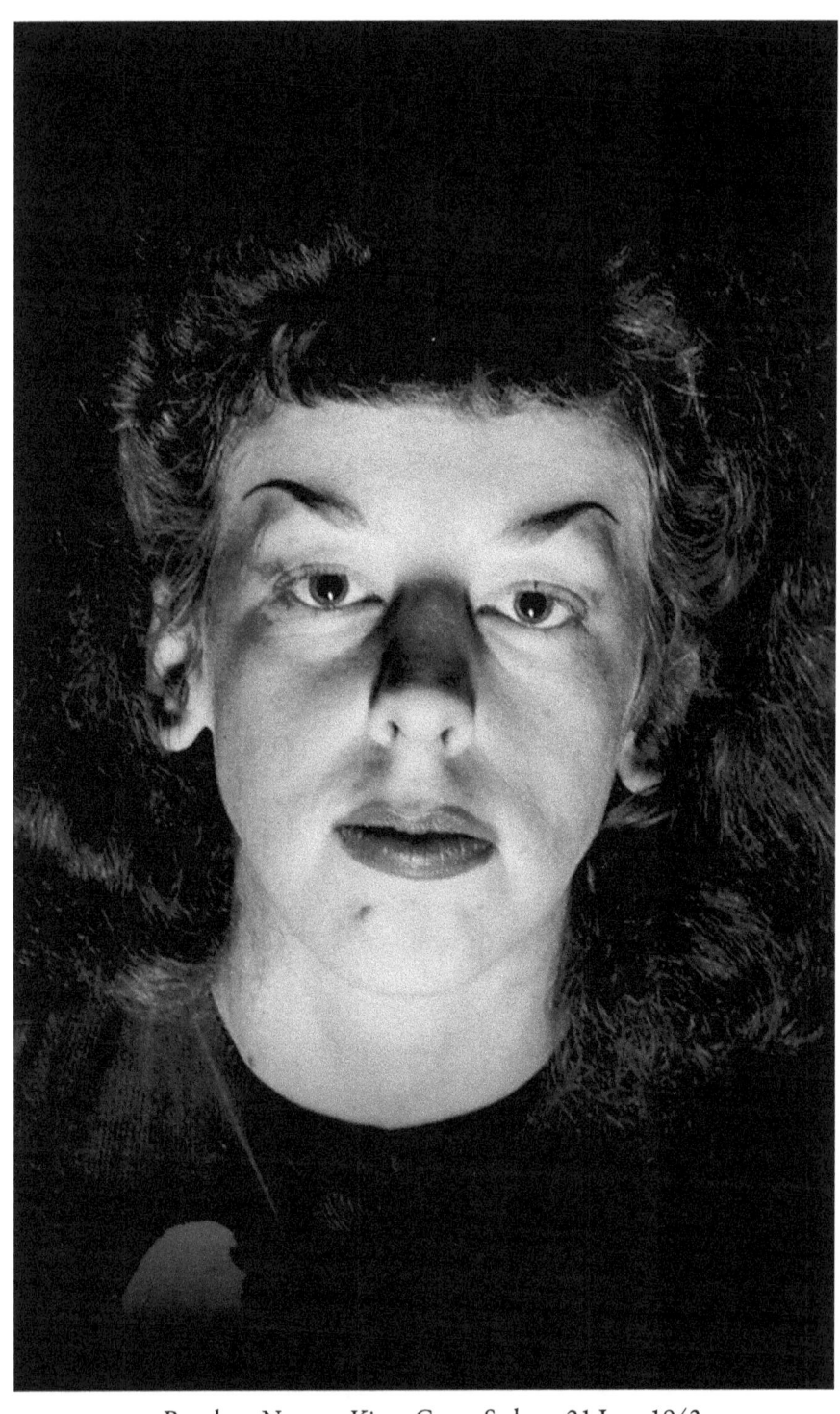

Rosaleen Norton, Kings Cross, Sydney, 21 June 1943.
By Ivan, for PIX Magazine, from photographic negative,
State Library of New South Wales.

Chapter Six

Rosaleen Norton
The Witch of King's Cross
(d. 1979)

𝕴n Sonia Bible's 2021 documentary *The Witch of King's Cross* the late painter, seer and Scientologist John Martensen describes Rosaleen Norton's raucous 38th birthday party in October 1955, which took place at her flat in the bohemian King's Cross area of Sydney. Fuelled by Cinzano Rosso and green ginger wine (her favourite), the revellers began partying at 4 o'clock in the afternoon, with festivities rolling on through the night until, as Martensen remembers, at 2pm the following day, "there's a tramp, tramp, tramp on the stairs. The coppers are coming." Having long been harrassed by the police on account of their "vagrancy", Norton and her partner Gavin Greenlees were quite possibly unsurprised. This time, however, the charge was a different one - "the abominable crime of buggery", as described in Section 79 of New South Wales' Crimes Act 1900:

> *'whosoever commits the abominable crime of buggery, or bestiality, with mankind, or with any animal, shall be liable to penal servitude for life, or any term not less than 5 years.'*

As Martensen points out in the documentary, "that's the only crime in the whole book, the law book, that has an adjective describing it". The evidence consisted of photographs, some of which depicted Norton and Greenlees engaged in sex-magical acts of flagellation and knife play; images which had been stolen by two members of their Pan-Hecate coven with the intent of making £200 through a sale to the gaudy Sydney *Sun* newspaper. Though the couple were acquitted,

Greenlees never truly recovered and spent much of the remainder of his life incarcerated in psychiatric institutions with a diagnosis of schizophrenia.

The life of visionary artist and witch Rosaleen Norton - 'Roie' to her friends - was punctuated by devastating entanglements with the criminal justice system. Greenlees wasn't the only loved one estranged from her as a result of arcane laws, as we shall see. Like Sybil Leek, Norton was a media sensation, but her persecution was undeniably more brutal. As a proudly queer, sexually liberated woman she was harangued daily in the street during the height of her infamy, charged numerous times for vagrancy and obscenity, and ended her life a virtual recluse. Norton's story lies at the intersection of issues which continue to be of prime importance in the present day: religious freedom, censorship, queer freedom, sexual liberation and women's rights. Mottled by Australia's barbarously conservative governance at the time, her life was one of tragedy and epiphany. It's rather appropriate that she was born during a thunderstorm.

Raised in an Anglican family with two sisters, Norton moved from Dunedin in New Zealand to Sydney, Australia, when she was eight years old. This location better suited her father - a cousin of the English composer Ralph Vaughan Williams - who was away at sea much of the time. Her relationship with her mother was fraught and for a long period she lived largely in a tent in the garden with insects as her friends and guardians. Expelled from school aged 14, Norton went on to study art at East Sydney Technical College under the renowned sculptor Raynor Hoff. Also a talented writer, she began publishing horror stories in *Smith's Weekly* in her mid-teens and was eventually taken on as a staff writer for the tabloid. She persuaded the editor Frank Marien to let her branch out into illustration, but her work was so morbidly gory that she was eventually shown the door. In *Pan's Daughter: The Magical World of Rosaleen Norton* (2016), Neville Drury describes one such drawing for the publication:

> '*The first drawing she offered Marien showed a number of women sitting in a circle on some grass, biting their babies and laughing their heads off. It was hardly the type of humour he had in mind.*'

By this point, the young artist's interests had already taken a turn towards the occult. According to Doreen Valiente, Norton claimed to have taken an oath of allegiance to the nature god Pan at the age of 13, during a ritual which involved the use of joss sticks, wine from her parents' collection, leaves and a little of her own blood. This ceremony seems to have been inspired not merely by reading of such things, but rather by her own insights or what might be deemed in contemporary magical communities as 'unverified personal gnosis' (UPG). Valiente notes how this intuitive form of magic "seems to indicate an unconscious memory from a previous incarnation as a witch". On Norton's part, she regarded herself as a born witch and flaunted physical proof of her otherly blood by drawing attention to "witch-marks" on her body: pointed ears, two blue dots on her left knee, and an extra muscle she possessed between her armpit and waist.

Following the death of her mother - and her dismissal from *Smith's Weekly* - Norton left a note for her family and headed off into the world alone. She found work as an artist's model, including for the eminent Norman Lindsay, whose female nudes were rather controversial at the time. She married briefly, though following the war the young couple broke up. It was during the war that Norton began experimenting with self-hypnosis; a set of techniques which she discovered led to extra sensory perceptions, visions, and the possibility for automatic drawing. Her day job at the magazine *Pertinent* brought her into contact with the poet Gavin Greenlees, who would eventually become her lover and magical ally. In 1949 the pair travelled to Melbourne and, with the assistance of Greenlees' connections, Norton held an exhibition at the University of Melbourne which foretold much of her later problems with the law. In an experience which somewhat mirrors that of Marjorie Cameron, two days following the exhibition's opening police removed four paintings they deemed obscene - *Witches' Sabbath*, *Lucifer*, *Triumph*, and *Individuation*. Norton was charged for this supposed crime, though won in court and was awarded compensation. This was a landmark case in Australia - the prosecution of a female artist - and a media scandal inevitably ensued. The fact that Norton claimed in court to have participated in the sex-magical activities on display in her paintings, and that she was visited by the fantastical beings that her art brought to life, was an act of great bravery given the culture of intensive censorship spearheaded by Australia's Prime Minister.

Upon returning to Sydney, Norton and Greenlees took on a flat in King's Cross, where Norton would earn - and eventually embrace - the moniker of "Witch of King's Cross". There was a strong beatnik feel to the neighbourhood, which for the most part only truly came to life after sundown. Queers, artists, sex workers and poets paraded the streets and spent all night drinking, dancing and chatting in the numerous cafes that spanned the area. The couple, like many others, were repeatedly harassed by the police for "vagrancy", which really amounted to no more than the so-called crime of unemployment. In order to escape jail, they were forced to seek work, and were rescued in this regard by the publisher Walter Glover, who offered them employment as his assistants. Recognising their talent, Glover commissioned the pair to write a book which would become *The Art of Rosaleen Norton* (1952), banned in the US and subject to censorship in Australia. Before atrocities were claimed of it, however, Norton had proudly sent copies to Albert Einstein, C.S. Lewis, Gerald Gardner and Carl Jung, revealing her confidence in the project. The charge of obscenity wagered at Glover rendered him bankrupt, yet the book drew the attention of the high society orchestral conductor Sir Eugene Goossens who, enamoured, sent a letter to Norton who invited him to tea. The two began an impassioned affair, with the trio of Norton, Greenlees and Goosens conducting a variety of sex-magical rituals together.

In 1956, not long after Norton and Greenlees' flat had been raided, Goossens was stopped by customs officers and arrested at Sydney airport upon his return from a trip to Europe. The prohibited goods he was accused of importing included rubber masks and pornographic photographic material depicting ritualistic activities involving Norton and Greenlees. Admitting his "unsavoury" appetites, Goosens was levied a fine and discarded from polite society (as was Norton). He returned to England to live the remainder of his life in disgrace. Norton was devastated. In apposite response she began to embrace the media hysteria, taking matters into her own hands. Like Leek before her, she posed in her appropriately cave-like home, adorned with her occult paintings, and the witch herself complete with pointy hat. She too, attempted to sculpt the media furore to more favourable ends, even going so far as to author autobiographical articles in the newspapers which had served her so poorly.

In her writings, and despite her sympathy for the witches being hounded in England at the time, Norton was always at pains to assert that her ends never included the furthering of the Witch Cult's cause:

> 'I do not wish to propagate any cult (even the Witch Cult), change society, establish a "better world" for others etc. ... I have what I prefer to describe as a function rather than a "message" or a "mission" (words which I detest). The function is that of focus and catalyst in relation to certain forces, situations, and people - and this function is best served by my performing my own personal will, and not caring a damn about effects good or bad upon other people'
> - Thorn in the Flesh: A Grim-memoire (2009).

It was with nature - rather than humanity - that Norton predominantly identified. Although she exchanged letters with Gerald Gardner, she paid little heed to the beliefs or political dynamics of Wicca, instead suggesting that their all-too human ceremonies rely upon the power of the human group rather than, for example, the "Abhuman Familiar". In a text collected in *Thorn in the Flesh*, Norton writes, "I feel an identification and natural unity with the traditional Folk-lore witch that I don't feel with the "Wiccan" [...] The Wiccan Gods...they seem to be mainly a kind of summing up of, respectively, All Men (the God) and All Women (The Goddess) instead of Beings in themselves having correspondences".

Keith Richmond, in his Introduction to *Thorn in the Flesh*, writes that Norton identified most closely with Not-Man, going by her own definitions. From this we can surmise that her positioning within the spheres of existence in some ways absolved her from the guilt of Greenlees, Glover and Goossens' fates. Richmond writes that:

> *'Rosaleen Norton taught that there were two quite distinct astral realms: the Human Astral, and the Elemental Astral. These had different vibratory rates, and were set, as it were, at ninety degrees to each other. Each contained a group of planes that together formed one of the two Great Orders of Being: that of Man and that of "Not-Man" (Pan/Nature); which together made up the Planetary entity'.*

Norton, Richmond argues, existed beyond planetary consciousness. She understood that the true Fallen Angel, as summarised in Madeline Montalban's Lucifer, was mankind itself, and that humanity was "held in the grip of a self-inflicted madness, which reversed back upon itself everything positive that it attempted to create". In this sense nature - as depicted by Pan - had no option but to become an adversary of humankind. Given the ongoing punishments she was subjected to as a result of her difference, it makes sense that Norton should attempt to disavow herself of humanity. Whilst it is true that Greenlees, Glover and Goossens suffered due to their connections with Norton, it is very clear that she was not to blame for their horrific experiences of ostracisation (mental, financial and societal). Rather, these men were victims of cruelly conservative politicians and lawmakers in possession of bigoted approaches to religious, artistic and sexual freedoms. Norton was a victim of these lawmakers too. Valiente writes in *The Rebirth of Witchcraft* (1989) that, "Rosaleen Norton was a trail-blazer, and she suffered the usual fate of those who try to introduce new ideas into society, namely to be persecuted and misunderstood". Yet again, wise Valiente hits the nail on the head.

Norton believed that her form of traditional witchcraft - what she called "The Goat Fold" - had roots in Britain and had been an export, along with convicts and emigrants, to Australia. These roots folded back upon themselves through the return passage of an initiatory text by Norton - titled *The First Knowledge* - via her student and fellow queer witch Leslie Roberts, across the pond and into Valiente's hands. Norton's text was then given, by Valiente, to a British Gardnerian High Priestess. It is quite possible that *The First Knowledge* is still used in some covens in Britain today. We can hope that the rebellious spirit of Norton's magic is an inheritance too. As for humanity? We continue to live through its ongoing war against Nature; that much is certain.

The Mother, Mirra Alfassa, in Pondicherry (24 April 1950).
Photographed by Henri Cartier-Bresson.

Chapter Seven

Mirra Alfassa
The Mother
(d. 1973)

> 'Her yoga was to tear down the barrier that separates heaven and earth by defeating the Lord of Death, through breaking the habituated belief that exists in every cell of the body that all life must end in death and dissolution. Ultimately, her goal was to transform and spiritualise matter.'
> ~ Stephen Lerner on Mirra Alfassa, in *Integral Review* (2013)

In this chapter we shall eventually travel eastwards to India, but the story of Mirra Alfassa - yogi, mystic and founder of the experimental utopian town Auroville - begins in 1878, amongst the bourgeoisie of Paris. Alfassa's birthplace was Boulevard Haussman, later home to Marcel Proust and now the site of the grand department store Galeries Lafayette. Her Egyptian mother and Turkish father, both of Jewish heritage, had emigrated only a short time earlier with their son Mattéo. The family were initially comfortable - employing an English nanny to look after the children - but their status changed in the wake of the 1892 Panama Scandal which rendered her father bankrupt. By this time, Alfassa had long been a practising occultist: "I practised occultism when I was twelve. But I was never afraid. I was afraid of nothing". Meditation and trance-work seemed to come naturally to her as a child; formative skills in her development as a megalithic figure in the history of both yoga and the occult.

At the age of 15, like several of the women in this book, Alfassa began formally training as an artist. She studied at the private art school Académie Julian in Montmartre for four years and went on to marry the painter Henri Morisset in 1897. The couple made their home near the Académie, with a footbridge to their studio, as well as keeping a country house on the Loire. Given these acquisitions we can assume their affluence at this time. Their son André was born in 1898, but this did not prevent Alfassa from exhibiting works during his early childhood; her paintings were accepted by the Salon d'Automne in three consecutive years, showing alongside works by luminaries such as Matisse, Cézanne, Renoir and Bonnard. Up until this period of her life Alfassa had been a strict atheist: "all I knew was the God of the religious, God as men have created him; and I didn't want him at any price. I denied his existence, but with the certitude that if such a God did exist, I detested him!" Having been given a copy of the *Bhagavad Gita* by Theosophist Jnanendra Nath Chakravarti, she was beginning to cultivate her own sense of the Divine; the "interior God". Her worldview, and life, were to change irrevocably.

It was during these early years as an artist that Alfassa first made contact with the Cosmic Movement which had been established in Algeria by the Polish Jewish Kabbalist Max Théon, and based upon esoteric cosmological information channelled by his wife Alma. Initially involved in one of the Movement's discussion groups, Alfassa met the Théons through her brother and she eventually became editor of their journal *Cosmic Review*. Over the course of two trips to the Théons' home in Tlemcen, Algeria, Alfassa's psychic skills came into their own; her realisations came thick and fast in seemingly awe-inspiring company. In Georges van Vreckhem's 2004 biography of Alfassa, the poet and playwright describes Alma and Max as two powerful magicians for whom even mundane activities were gateways to occult faculty-building: "when Alma wanted her slippers, she fixed her gaze upon them and they obediently came shuffling towards her". There was nothing haphazard about the Théon's approach to magic, and their systematic approach rubbed off on Alfassa, who states that:

> *'I always compare occultism with chemistry, for it is the same kind of knowledge as that of chemistry regarding material things. It is a knowledge of invisible forces, their various vibrations, their interrelations [...] There are combinations as explosive as certain chemical combinations.'*

Alfassa's second visit to Tlemcen proved particularly eventful - almost deadly, in fact - as van Vreckhem explains:

> *'In some world visited by Mirra during her exteriorization [out-of-body] under the direction of [Max] Théon, she found the 'Mantra of Life'. This is the formula by which one can give life and also take it, create life and also destroy it. 'This mantra was shut away, sealed, with my name on it in Sanskrit. I didn't know Sanskrit at that time, but he did'. Still, Mirra was aware that it was Sanskrit, told Théon so and started to describe the characters to him. Théon, for some reason, 'got very interested.' He told Mirra to break the seal and tell him what was hidden there. Then 'something in me knew at once', and she refused to tell him.*
>
> *This made Théon very angry and his anger cut the cord. Mirra was dead. Théon, because Mirra had been able to warn him in the nick of time, became frightened and used all his occult knowledge and powers to pull her back into her material body.'*

As Godwin, Chanel and Deveney note in *The Hermetic Brotherhood of Luxor* (1995), Théon and his relationship with Alma - and, perhaps, given the above anecdote, Mirra - may belong to the tradition of "spiritual research conducted by a man controlling a psychically gifted woman". Certainly this trope is so well grounded to now have taken root in popular culture too: we see the dynamic played out between the siblings Margaret and Archibald Campbell in season three of the television series *Outlander* (2017). Whatever their relationship, and despite her near-death experience, Alfassa and Max

Théon travelled across the Mediterranean together upon treacherous seas which Alfassa claimed to have calmed, upon the instruction of Théon, with her developing occult powers. After their trip, it is uncertain whether they ever saw each other again. Alma died a short while later in 1908 and her husband never truly recovered from this great loss. Max sank into a long depressive episode, disbanding the Cosmic Movement and shutting himself away until his own death in 1927.

Alfassa's involvement in the Cosmic Movement lasted five years, during which time her artistic career and marriage dissolved. She divorced Morisset in the year that Alma died, and began to mingle with a new set of artists, composers and spiritual seekers in Paris. Her approach became increasingly holistic and her goals lofty - she was disinterested in fashionable practices such as automatic writing, and dismissed the use of 'elementals', which she deemed as 'small vital entities', that made fools of the humans engaging with them. For Alfassa, it seems, such practices were flippant and showy. One of her followers, the philosopher Kireet Joshi, describes Alfassa's dedication to her spiritual path over the coming decade:

> '...these ten years were a period of intensive mental studies for the Mother. This meant a mental development in all its comprehensiveness: the study of all philosophies, all the juggling of ideas in their smallest details - entering into systems and understanding them [...] She came to the conclusion that all ideas are true, that a synthesis had to be made, and that there is something luminous and true beyond the synthesis.'

Amidst this intensive period of study, reflection and practice, Alfassa met Sri Aurobindo - a political revolutionary-turned philosopher yogi - for the first time during a trip to Pondicherry with her second husband, Paul Richard. This coming together marked a culmination in both of their paths up until this point. Alfassa stayed in India for over a year, only returning to France because of the outbreak of the First World War. From there she and her husband travelled to Japan at the behest of the French. Alfassa continued to write and give talks on spiritual matters, engaging with the culture of her new country of residence as well as the broader world's catastrophic struggles. The following passage from her *Collected Works* demonstrates her capacity for capturing the zeitgeist and placing it in relationship to her own beliefs:

> *'Nietzsche made the mistake we said we ought to avoid: his superman is but a man aggrandised, magnified, in whom Force has become super-dominant, crushing under its weight all the other attributes of man. Such cannot be our ideal. We see too well at present whither leads the exclusive worshipping of Force—to the crimes of the strong and the ruin of continents.*
>
> *No, the way to supermanhood lies in the unfolding of the ever-perfect Spirit. All would change, all would become easy if man could once consent to be spiritualised. The higher perfection of the spiritual life will come by a spontaneous obedience of spiritualised man to the truth of his own realised being, when he has become himself, found his own real nature; but this spontaneity will not be instinctive and subconscient as in the animal, but intuitive and fully, integrally conscient.'*

Four years later the couple, along with Dorothy Hodgson (a friend and follower of Alfassa later known as Dutta), returned to India to take up residence near Sri Aurobindo. Richard took off traveling around a year later (the pair eventually divorced) and shortly after his departure there was a great rainstorm that threatened to do away with the women's house. And so, Alfassa and Dutta moved into Aurobindo's home. The guru considered Alfassa an equal, proclaiming her 'The Mother'; possibly in response to tensions in the bustling household upon the arrival of these two female outsiders.

The Sri Aurobindo Ashram was founded in 1926, with day-to-day management and spiritual guidance undertaken by Alfassa. At the core of Alfassa and Aurobindo's teachings and practices, collectively known as Integral yoga, was the aim of developing the capacity to identify oneself with the Divine - the God (or Absolute) within, and to manifest it. Alfassa emphasised that God has a rather wicked sense of humour, and that we would do well to keep ours lively too:

> '...we are all acting a play, but we do not know what the play is, nor where it is going, nor where it comes from, nor what is as a whole [...] Our knowledge is imperfect. And so we worry! But when one knows everything, one can no longer worry, one smiles - He must be having great fun, but we...And yet we are given the full power to amuse ourselves like him'

For Alfassa, our material world as it is might be imperfect, but above all it is sacred in its own way:

> 'It is a mistake to make "matter" a synonym for obscurity and ignorance. And the material world too is not the only world in which we live: it is rather one of many in which we exist simultaneously, and in one way the most important of them all. For this world of matter is the points of concentration of all the worlds: it is the field of concretisation of all the worlds; it is the place where all the worlds will have to manifest. At present it is disharmonious and obscure, but that is only an accident, a false start. One day it will become beautiful, rhythmic, full of light; for that is the consummation for which it was made.'

We might find ourselves wondering what had become of Alfassa's son during these years. Left behind with his father's family, we might be inclined to sneer about Alfassa's mantle as The Mother. Yet Alfassa recognised that maternity has many guises and operates at many levels; few (if any) of which are biological. In an address titled *To the Women of Japan*, she explains:

> *'True maternity begins with the conscious creation of a being, with the willed shaping of a soul coming to develop and utilize a new body...The work really commences when, by the power of thought and will, we conceive and create a character capable of manifesting the ideal.'*

Commenting on this seeming disjuncture between Alfassa's private and public lives, the scholar of religious studies Nika Kuchuk notes that Alfassa seems to be leveraging different aspects of being the Mother against one another, and in doing so, "hits on some key significations of motherhood, materiality and gender as sociocultural and religious constructions." With reference to the fact that, for Alfassa, transformed humanity will be androgynous, Kuchuk goes on to argue that underlying The Mother's discourse might be "attempts to pluralise this space, upsetting ingrained binaries and, at the same time, maintaining the body as the ground of experience". In this sense, Alfassa is "occupying the archetype and resisting it".

The magic of Mirra Alfassa was the magic of heroic and monumental hope. Hope for an enlightened and transcendent humanity that has its roots firmly in the present but its gaze towards the future. We find this in her love of humour, possibility, and radicalism. We find this in her lack of ego. In 1968 she went on to manifest her grandest ambition: the experimental township of Auroville. This project was driven by a desire for diverse people to live harmoniously, and according to their 1965 declaration, "above all creeds, all politics, and all nationalities". In collaboration with the French architect Roger Anger, Alfassa created the Galaxy Plan - a design based on sacred geometry which envisioned and enabled a multi-faceted community comprising green belt land, an industrial zone, cultural zone, residential zone, and so on, plotted on an evocative spiral grid. Today Auroville's population stands at almost 3000. Commended and endorsed by UNESCO as a project of importance to the future of humanity, the Auroville Solar Bowl enables the preparation of vegetarian food for over 1000 people in the community every day. Auroville also facilitates research into permaculture, water biodynamics, eco-city models, healthcare and sustainability. Impressively, it remains one of the few late-1960s utopian visions for communal living still in existence. Though by no means perfect, Auroville stands as a major feat of design, creativity and humanity.

Mirra Alfassa's ambitions and achievements were vast. She counted Gandhi and the Dalai Lama amongst her esteemed visitors; her commanding leadership skills and spiritual advice were greatly sought after. It feels right that she left her body peacefully, in November 1973, and was laid to rest beside her spiritual partner, Sri Aurobindo.

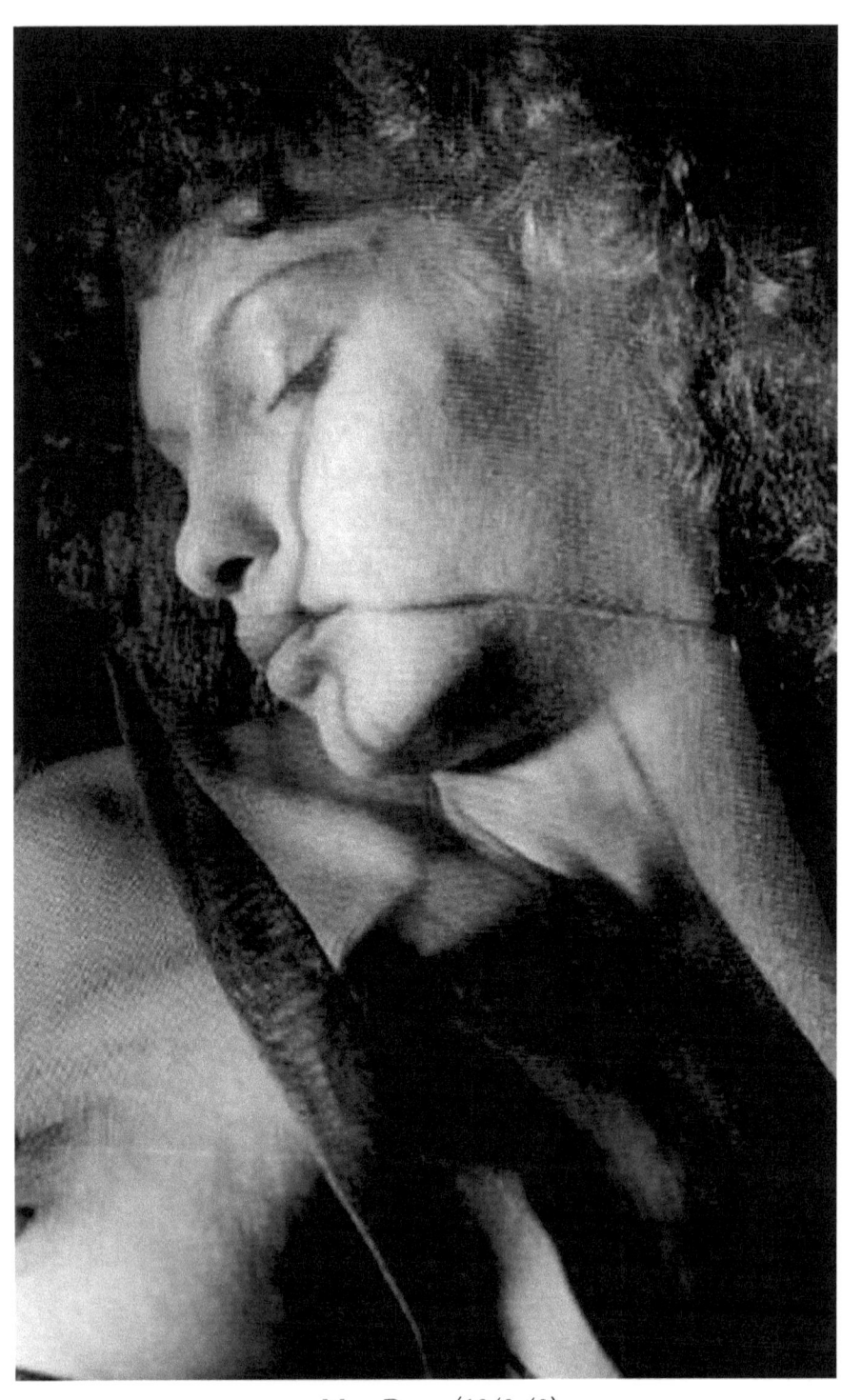

Maya Deren (1942-43).
Photographed by Alexandr Hackenschmied.

Chapter Eight

Maya Deren
Sorceress of the Screen
(d. 1961)

माया • (māyā) ~ Vedic.

1. *art, wisdom, inhuman or supernatural power*
2. *love, affection*
3. *(Classical Sanskrit) illusion, deception, trickery, demonic magic*

𝕵ust as Mirra Alfassa became The Mother, the adoption of a new name - one's 'true' name - is undertaken across many cultures as an initiation rite. Perhaps Eleonora Deren nurtured this thought in her mind when she became Maya Deren in 1943; the same year that she set out on a filmmaking journey which would establish her as one of the major proponents of the 20th century avant-garde, eventually mentoring luminaries such as Marjorie Cameron's filmmaking associates Curtis Harrington and Kenneth Anger. Deren would also gain international renown as an ethnographer (and practitioner) of Haitian Vodou, with her book *Divine Horsemen: The Living Gods of Haiti* (1953) earning stellar praise from Joseph Campbell: "this little volume is the most illuminating introduction that has yet been rendered to the whole marvel of the *Haitian mystères* as "facts of the mind"."

Deren was a youthful polymath with several degrees who wrote poetry and prose, lectured, made films and demonstrated a fierce entrepreneurial spirit in order to fund her creative endeavours. Nevertheless, there was a frenzy which accompanied her, with wild rumours that she had displaced Vodou spirits, or perhaps become permanently possessed. The filmmaker Stan Brakhage famously described a moment in which he watched Deren fling - with awesome, eerie strength - a large refrigerator across a room during a rage, and in the collection *Maya Deren and the American Avant-Garde* (2001), Brakhage's former wife Jane Wodening recalls:

> *'And so, when all the people were gathered at the Reception, Maya Deren became possessed by the voodoo god Papa Loco. She went into the kitchen and she started to roar and she picked up the refrigerator that weighed several hundred pounds and she threw it across the kitchen [...] Members of the Wedding who understood voodoo stayed with her there, got her into bed where she sat roaring and demanding things to be brought to her. And the way she roared was she would roll her head from side to side and roar with each breath.'*

Deren's hectic life came abruptly to a halt at the age of 44, following a cerebral haemorrhage. A tragic event, which was possibly caused by the amphetamines prescribed by Deren's doctor, Max Jacobson. 'Dr. Feelgood', as he was known, is understood to have engaged in dangerously generous prescribing practices when it came to his high-profile clients. For many onlookers, however, Deren's early death was further proof of her exposure - and proximity - to the uncanny. This convergence of magical unrealities and mundane life are threaded throughout Deren's oeuvre of films which, quite astonishingly given her influence, amounts to a mere 78 minutes of total running time. Nevertheless, the vast and sprawling legend of this screen sorceress endures.

In 1917, Eleanora Derenkovskaya was born in Kyiv, Soviet Ukraine, to a psychologist father and a mother who had trained in both music and dance. The family relocated to New York (shortening their surname to Deren) when Eleanora was five years old, escaping the anti-Semitic pogroms committed by the anti-communist White

Volunteer Army. After attending an international high school in Geneva, Deren returned to New York to study journalism and political science, becoming heavily involved in the Trotskyist movement and earning the role of National Secretary of the Young People's Socialist League (YPSL). In this swift ascension to the upper echelons of the YPSL we see something of the willfulness, passion and ambition that enabled Deren to find funding for her creative work; seeking connections and promoting herself to achieve her goals.

It was through politics that she met Gregory Bardacke, who she married at the age of 18. The young couple moved to New York City following his graduation, where she herself later graduated from New York University with a degree in literature. Her marriage to Bardacke was short-lived - she separated from him at this time, and they divorced three years later. Academically brilliant, Deren continued her education at Smith College, where she gained a master's degree in literature, writing her thesis on the French Symbolists' influence on Anglo-American modernist poetry. It was poetry and writing, rather than film, which engaged Deren's heart during this period and she pursued her ambitions whilst working as a freelance secretary.

It was perhaps by means of this work as a secretary that she first came into contact with the occult and her life's passion, Haitian Vodou. In 1939 she assisted William Seabrook as researcher and secretary during the writing of his book *Witchcraft - Its Power in the World Today* (1940). Judith Noble tells a tale from this time in *Frames Cinema Journal* (Issue 16):

> *'Deren's experience with Seabrook ended bizarrely when he unsuccessfully tried to make her participate in a series of sadomasochistic sexual rituals at his home... She later described how these centered on the use of a "witch's cradle"* [the title of Deren's unfinished 1943 film]*, a device intended to induce trance and vision.'*

Noble suggests that Deren likely learned a great deal about witchcraft and magic - in both the European and Afro-Caribbean traditions - from Seabrook, regardless of whether or not she partook in his private ritual endeavours. This education was continued during Deren's time spent travelling in a managerial role with dancer and anthropologist Katherine Dunham and her Afro-American dance troupe. Dunham had studied Vodou in Haiti and incorporated ritual motifs into her work, embodying the practices of the African diaspora in the Americas. Deren's fascination with Afro-Caribbean spirituality and ritual seems to have preceded her time with the choreographer. In *Maya Deren: Incomplete Control* (2014), Sarah Keller notes that Deren sought Dunham out, successfully persuading the latter to employ her. Given that this was during the Jim Crow era of racial segregation in the US, we can make assumptions about the progressive nature of Deren's politics.

In 1942 the troupe's tour landed in Los Angeles, and it was at a Hollywood cocktail party that Deren met the Czech filmmaker and photographer Alexander Hackenschmied (later Hammid), who became her second husband. They settled in Laurel Canyon, collaborating the following year on Deren's fourteen minute magnum opus, *Meshes of the Afternoon* (1943). Situated somewhere between a dream sequence and a nightmare, the film depicts a woman disoriented in both space and time, haunted (or perhaps possessed) within the quotidian-melodramatic aura of a Hollywood bungalow. These two planes - the all-American workaday environment and spiritual possession - were to rub along together for the remainder of Deren's life.

Though Deren abhorred the label 'Surrealist' being applied to her work, she was no doubt impacted (if not influenced) by the movement. During her time spent in Greenwich Village, New York, she immersed herself in an arts scene populated by European émigrés including heavyweight Surrealists such as André Breton and Max Ernst. The appropriation and adoption of occult ideas was common amongst those on the scene. Perhaps Deren's repudiation of the term 'Surrealist' signals that she was not so much decontextualising the occult (in the manner of many surrealists), as deeply enmeshed in some of its beliefs. Writing about film in *Mademoiselle* (January, 1946) she states:

> *'Here was a medium which, instead of being bound by the astronomy of clocks and calendars, could make manifest the astronomy of the heart and mind - that which knows an evening as endless, or the walk back always being shorter than the first walk there... we act and suffer and love according to what we imagine to be true, whether it is really true or not. And since the cinema seemed peculiarly qualified to project those inner realities, I had always been impatient with what I felt was a criminal neglect of that potent magic power.'*

A restless spirit, who left in her wake an abundance of incomplete films and unedited material, Deren was as experimental as an alchemist in her approaches to both life and work. Following the end of World War II, many of her friends returned to Europe and the vibrant scene of artists that she had flourished amongst began to fade away. In 1947, Deren divorced Hammid and set off for Haiti to pursue her interest in Vodou, funded by the Guggenheim Fellowship. This was the first time that the fellowship had been awarded to a filmmaker. There, Deren not only studied the religion, but became initiated into it too, extending herself far beyond the parameters of her funding remit. As Noble notes, "From this point on, she would consider the practice of Voudon to be the most important aspect of her life". Deren eventually asked to film some of the ceremonies in which she had taken part. She writes about this conversation with a Vodou priest in *Divine Horsemen: The Living Gods of Haiti* (1953):

> *'I spoke to him of my desire to capture the beauty and the significance of the ceremonies, so that the rest of the world might become aware. He understood virtually nothing of cinema and I was uncertain of his reaction, since his own standing in the community could be jeopardised by such a permission [...] He hesitated but a moment. Then, offering his hand as one would to a colleague or collaborator, he said: "Each one serves in his own fashion".'*

For Deren, practising Vodou was a transformative, world-view shaking experience. Through ritual experiences such as possession ceremonies, she came to understand the religion as offering possibilities for an enlarged perspective of the self, with something like an expansive, ego-destabilising depersonalisation taking place. In *Divine Horsemen* she notes that,

> *'... to be made aware, once more, that man is of divine origin and is the issue of and heir to an uncounted multitude of hearts and minds; that at the root of the universe the great imperturbable principles of cosmic good endure; and that even under his torn shirt, his hunger, the failures of his wit and the errors of his heart, his very blood harbors these monumental loa [Vodou spirits] - is to experience the major blessing with which possession rewards men's dedicated service.'*

Deren returned to Haiti several times after her initial eight month stay. In between visits she appeared on television and radio to address common misperceptions of Vodou; attempting to undo dangerous, often racist stereotypes that deigned the religion 'black magic' or 'hocus pocus'. This was a political act driven by moral imperative - even within Haiti itself Vodou had been suppressed, denied and ridiculed. Like Sybil Leek, Deren was eloquent and convincing, as well as eccentric and alluring; unruly hair and handmade European-style clothing cut a fascinating aesthetic for American audiences.

Whilst Deren spoke openly about Vodou, there is something shy in the way she buries the core of her magical practice at the very end of her 1953 book. In a chapter titled *The White Darkness*, she writes of her personal experience of spirit possession, recording a night in Haiti when the *loa* entered her head. She describes how she sensed herself to be vulnerable and sought to overcome the possession upon spotting its early signs, noting that, "The loa can come like this, without warning, as a wind". Deren debates running away from the ceremony but realises "it is not fair to stay only when it is easy." Her experience of possession is defined by terror:

> *'I am caught in this cylinder, this well of sound. There is nothing anywhere except this. There is no way out. The white darkness moves up the veins of my leg like a swift tide rising [...] It is too much, too bright, too white for me; this is its darkness. "Mercy!" I scream within me [...] I am sucked down and exploded upward at once. That is all."*

Hidden away in the chapter's footnotes, we find reflections upon the religion and its practices as they relate to her personally. Here, Deren's true dedication to the path of Vodou is revealed:

> *'Is this to say that I believe in Voudon and in Erzulie [feminine spirits]? [...] In the context of Voudon, such a question did not occur to me. I would say that, as a metaphysical and ritualistic structure* Voudon is a fact.'

When at home, Deren also wrote, lectured boldly about film to rooms largely devoid of other women, and offered mentorship to young filmmakers such as Curtis Harrington, who threw Deren a party following her lecture at Club Renaissance in Hollywood. In his biography of Marjorie Cameron, Spencer Kansa captures the convergence of Deren and Cameron that night, as told by the gonzo journalist (and master of schlock Hollywood memoirs) John Gilmore:

> *'She [Deren] was used to being the centre of attention, and was in typically high spirits that evening, dancing wildly on a table in Curtis' apartment while Gilmore and fellow actor Russ Tamblyn banged away on bongo drums. In a telling image, Gilmore recollects catching sight of Cameron at the party, hunched up and smoking in a corner, studying Deren intently. Babalon may have been eclipsed by the Vodoun Queen that night, but she didn't leave the party without planting a goodbye kiss on Deren's lips as she left.'*

We can only wonder as to spoken communications between the two, whether or not further convergences occurred. It is certainly telling that at Cameron's memorial the Thelemite William Breeze and his girlfriend read from Deren's (unpublished) work *Lilith*.

Throughout her visits to Haiti, Deren filmed around 18,000 feet of tape, took one thousand still photographs and made fifty hours of audio recordings. Although she logged shot descriptions for 5,400 feet of film, she never completed the Haitian project she intended and the footage remained stored in a fire-proof box in her closet. Following Deren's death, her third husband Teiji Itō (who scored Deren's films and married her in 1960), along with his new wife Cherel Winett Itō, incorporated the footage into a film which took the title of Deren's book - *Divine Horsemen: Living Gods of Haiti* (1977).

Whilst the film undeniably offers fascinating insights into Deren's discoveries and the authentic practices of Vodou, viewers are left wondering how Deren might have brought the footage to life had she been able to complete the film herself. Keller rightly notes that "the whole of Deren's work - even long before her tragic end, even indeed from the very beginning - was always already marked by incompletion". This brings up a possible tension between art and magic, and the difference between the completion of a work of art and the conclusion of a magical working. The latter often being neither pretty, satisfying, nor designed (at least primarily) for human eyes.

Liminality and unresolved tensions populated not only Deren's work, but her life too. She belonged to multiple geographical locations and cultures, endured three marriages, was a Vodou initiate with Jewish roots, and remained an outspoken woman despite working within the heavily masculine world of film. Deren the artist-magician reminds us that the resolution of tensions is neither necessary nor desirable. Women, in particular, are so often told that they need something - usually a husband, or a baby - to complete them. But what if that focus, that dream, was shifted from one of completion to one of uncanny tension instead? This thrill, encapsulated ritualistically in just over an hour's worth of completed films, is Maya Deren's true legacy.

Pamela Colman Smith (1878 - 1951).
From the October 1912 issue of The Craftsman magazine.

Chapter Nine
Pamela Colman Smith
Tarot's High Priestess
(d. 1951)

𝔍n his 1907 volume *Bohemia in London*, author Arthur Ransome describes meeting Pamela Colman Smith (known to her friends as "Pixie") at one of her tipsy artist's salons:

> 'She was dressed in an orange-coloured coat that hung loose over a green skirt, with black tassels sewn all over the orange silk [...]. She welcomed us with a little shriek [...]. It was obviously an affectation, and yet seemed just the right manner of welcome from the strange little creature, "goddaughter of a witch and sister to a fairy," who uttered it.'

Encounters with Colman Smith typically described her exoticism, her childlike ethereality, yet also a healthy vigour. Throughout her life, such descriptions were peppered with bewilderment regarding her age, ethnicity, and sexuality. Colman Smith's vast body of work is similarly confounding. She made herself at home in the varied roles of artist, occultist, poet, designer, suffragist, folklorist, editor, publisher, and miniature-theatre maker. Most notably, she is famed as the illustrator of the Rider Waite Smith tarot deck - the most widely used and easily recognisable deck in the world today.

Born in 1878 to Brooklynite parents living in London, Pamela travelled widely throughout her youth, including stints in Jamaica which would inspire her later career as a performer of Jamaican folklore (under the mysteriously far-flung pseudonym 'Gelukiezanger'). Art and writing were in her maternal blood, and aged fifteen she went to study at New York's Pratt Institute where, according to Elizabeth Foley O'Connor, she was "widely regarded as a child prodigy". Indeed, she was prodigious in all senses of the word—both eerily impressive and otherworldly.

A move to London in 1900 was precipitated by her close friendship with the actress Ellen Terry. In a letter to her cousin with news of the move, Pamela practically yells "I am going home with Miss Terry?!!!!! Isant [sic] it lovely!!!!???!!!" Ellen ensured that Pamela quickly became embedded in London's rambunctiously colourful bohemian scene. Surrounded by artists, writers, actors and musicians, much of her initial work was in the theatre. She gamely performed in crowd scenes during one of the Lyceum Theatre's tours of the UK as well as adding costume and stage design to her oeuvre. W.B. Yeats was a welcome mentor and collaborator, offering advice and content when she launched *The Green Sheaf* in 1903—a magazine dedicated, somewhat characteristically, "to pleasure".

Like many—if not most—of Pamela's multifarious projects, the magazine was no commercial success. It seems that Pamela was a persistently enterprising but not entirely successful hustler. To supply *The Green Sheaf* with a stream of hand-colourists, she had set up a school for the purpose; it remains unknown as to whether any students actually enrolled. A sceptic might say that Pamela's enigmatically engineered persona was the product of a mind scheming after finances and fashions. She certainly made a habit of playing around with ambiguities surrounding her identity and ethnicity—perhaps even exploiting notions that she might be, for example, Japanese, during a time when the East was very much in vogue. Those more attuned to the art world might instead recognise Pamela as a cannily theatrical polymath, resourcefully scrabbling around to make an independent living.

Pamela's friendship with Yeats ultimately led towards her future renown as Arthur Waite's collaborator on the Rider Waite Smith deck. In 1901, guided by Yeats, 23-year-old Pamela joined the Hermetic Order of the Golden Dawn, an occult society dedicated to the pursuit of metaphysical knowledge through ritual and scholarship. The Order was filled to the brim with experimental thinkers and creatives such as Florence Farr, and Pamela's friend from the Lyceum, Bram Stoker ("Bramy Joker"). Never advancing beyond the second level of the Golden Dawn's many initiatory stages, Pamela skirted the fringes. Nonetheless, her artistic skills caught the attention of Waite:

> *'It seemed to some of us in the circle that there was a draughtswoman amongst us who, under proper guidance, could produce a tarot with an appeal to the world of art and a suggestion of the significance behind the Symbols.'*

In 1903 the Order splintered, with Waite's Rectified Order of the Golden Dawn seeking to explore a purely Christian mysticism, described by academic Helen Farley as "torturous". Pamela followed Waite (rather than Yeats, who also formed a new society), which is perhaps unsurprising given her later conversion to Catholicism. It was within this new configuration that Waite proposed the creation of a tarot deck. He credits Pamela with a certain naivety regarding occult symbolism, claiming that "the one thing she lacked was an interest in the meaning of it!" This dismissiveness of Pamela's scholarly capacities is perhaps predictable given the place in society that female artists occupied at the time. Nevertheless, it's possible that she enjoyed the Order for its pomp and ritual, not to mention the social aspect of the group—what could be more enticing to a young artist than a secret society comprising artists?

Despite writing to her editor Alfred Stieglitz that Waite's tarot project was "a big job for very little cash!" (she adored an exclamation mark), Pamela's turnaround was swift. She completed all 78 illustrations in just a few months for a flat fee, a sum sadly in keeping with her historically unacknowledged contribution to the deck. Whilst Waite focused his prescriptiveness on the symbolism of the tarot's Major Arcana (the "trump" cards), it's possible that he left the illustration of the Minor Arcana (the "pip" cards) to Pamela's uninhibited imagination. Secrecy was paramount within the Golden Dawn, and it is perhaps for this reason that Pamela never publicly discussed the meanings behind her tarot illustrations. Nonetheless, in a 1908 article titled "Should the Art Student Think?", she instructs budding artists in the way of creating and viewing art that applies equally well to tarot reading: "Use your wits, use your eyes. Perhaps you use your physical eyes too much and only see the mask. Find your eyes within, look for the door in the unknown country."

We might, upon closer examination, note that the figures in Pamela's tarot are often gender-ambiguous, reflecting the trend for short hair and masculine clothing common amongst her female friends at the time. Indeed, Pamela's friends often served as informal models on whom she based her illustrations - we can recognise the face of a young, boldly sociable Ellen Terry in the outwardly oriented Queen of Wands. The androgynous figures of her tarot add a dose of heft to suggestions of Pamela's queerness - she never married, had no children, and latterly spent 30 years with her companion Nora Lake. More than this, and regardless of her sexual orientation, the representation of gender neutrality points towards Pamela's future involvement with the pre-war suffragist movement, for which she designed propaganda posters as part of the artists' collective Suffrage Atelier. Her work for the movement is both astute and deeply witty—thoroughly undermining Waite's sense of her as largely surface-oriented.

Nature, too, is always close at hand in the Rider Waite Smith deck—from the Empress' lush garden and the robe of pomegranates, to the wild seas, mountains and creatures (both real and mythical) featured throughout the deck. Waite was fascinated by the Grail tradition, including Arthurian lore. This was a passion shared by Pamela. In youthful letters to her cousin she describes working on whimsical drawings of Merlin and Guinevere, and in 1899 visited Tintagel, the supposed site of Arthur's conception.

Waite's obsession with Christian mysticism is also widely apparent in the deck—from the Judgement card's overt references to the

Resurrection to The World card's Four Living Creatures of Ezekiel. Enthralled as she was by ritual, representation, and ceremony, Pamela converted to Roman Catholicism in 1911. Whilst conversion to or from Christianity was not uncommon within occult circles, some of her more bohemian friends treated her fresh piousness with disdain, and many ties were weakened or severed due to the perceived loss of Pamela's much lauded playfulness and verve. Following a stay with Pamela in 1913, Lily Yeats scathingly wrote that "she now has the dullest of friends, selected entirely because they are R.C., converts most of them, half-educated people, who want to see both eyes in a profile drawing."

Pamela eventually used a familial bequest to sign a lease on a property at the Lizard peninsula in Cornwall. There she and Nora would become caretakers for a chapel, whilst also providing retreat space for the clergy. Her later years were ones of quiet service and creativity–perhaps the end of the journey for an avid spiritual seeker, someone who championed communal inspiration above the patriarchal traditions of marriage and family. Despite ongoing attempts to revive her artistic career, Pamela died without funds in 1951. Pilgrims, fellow seekers, and tarot enthusiasts from across the globe continue to search for her unmarked pauper's grave; as notoriously problematic to pin down in death as she was in life.

Maria de Naglowska (1883-1936)
Portrait by Travis Simpkins (2022)

Chapter Ten

Maria de Naglowska
Satanic Woman
(d. 1936)

We now find ourselves in St Petersburg during the era of Grigori Yefimovich Rasputin - the mysterious Russian mystic who famously proved almost impossible to assassinate. It is 1883. The Russian Empire rules over 125 million people, though its hour is almost up. Affluent General Dmitry Stanislovovic Naglovskaja and aristocratic Katherine Kamaroff welcome their daughter Marija Dmitrevna Naglovskaja into the world. Despite an ever-chaste demeanour, "Maria de Naglowska" grows up to spout heretical ideas, to practise near-deadly sex-magical rituals, to translate Rasputin's biography, and to write many books detailing her Satanic beliefs with a view to educating her followers. So far we have met several women involved in sexual magic - both willingly, and perhaps unwittingly too. Maria de Naglowska reigns chief amongst their ancestors.

But for now Maria is an orphan, aged 12. General Naglovskaja has been poisoned by a member of the revolutionary Nihilist movement posing in the guise of a servant, and Katherine dies soon after, leaving Maria in the care of an aunt. A thorough classical education is provided courtesy of the Smolny Institute of Noble Maidens, where the focus is on - above all - a *moral* education. From youth Naglowska refuses to tow the line and falls in love with Jewish musician Moise Hopenko, eloping with him to Berlin and then Geneva, where they are married. At odds with Maria's family, they find themselves cut off from her wealth. The couple bear three children, though Moise sets off on a Palestinian pilgrimage never to return, leaving his wife to make her own living. Her exceptional schooling enables Naglowska to find work as a pedagogue, translator and journalist; three fields in which she excels throughout her life. Her rebellious streak rears its head again however, as scholar Michele Olsi writes of her appearance at a 1918 political conference:

> *'She exposed in this speech her libertarian position, and exhibited her opposition to the powers that ruled the roost in Europe at the time, Russia included. This act cost her prison, and later an expulsion from Geneva, for both her and her family.'*

One of her sons made it to Palestine to be with his father, whilst Naglowska and her other two children spent time in Bern and Basel before settling in Rome. It was in the Italian capital that she met the right-wing traditionalist philosopher and esotericist Julius Evola, proceeding to translate his poetry into French, as well as possibly embarking on an affair with him. This collaboration - whatever its full form may have taken - is unsurprising given the duo's intense mutual interest in sexual magic. Just as important as her encounter with Evola at this time, Naglowska was approached one day by an unnamed monk who handed her a drawing on cardboard. This simple diagram of a triangle set the course for Naglowska's calling as a leader, a philosopher, and a Satanic Woman.

The triangle represented the Trinity: with God the Father and the Son at two of the apexes, then the Holy Ghost's point labelled as *feminine*. This "Third Term of the Trinity" was, for Naglowska in this moment of epiphany, Woman. Naglowska believed that the eras of the Father (Judaism) and the Son (Christianity) had played out their usefulness, and that the coming age was that of Woman. This future would require and honour the reconciliation of opposites; the transformation, by means of purification, of darkness into light, Satan into God. Robert North writes of this process, in the context of the new religious movement Naglowska would go on to establish in Paris,

MARIA DE NAGLOWSKA: SATANIC WOMAN

'The purpose of her religion is to call upon the spirit of evil, not to combat it, but to deliver it, by purifying it through these rites for the good of humanity: it is this which she calls "the redemption of Satan."

It was 1929 when Naglowska arrived in Paris, her remaining son having travelled to Palestine and her daughter employed as a nurse. Unable to obtain a work permit, Naglowska lived in a hotel in Montparnasse and gave lectures on Satanism and sexual magic at cafes, swiftly gaining something of a following (possibly including William Seabrook, André Breton, Georges Bataille and Man Ray). According to Charles Sowerwine, one lecture at Club de Faubourg ended with the venue being charged with "outrage to public decency". Naglowska was billed for the event as "High Priestess of Love of the Temple of the Third Era". In 1932 she formed the Confrérie de la Flèche d'Or (Brotherhood of the Golden Arrow). The group's teachings, which required progressing through several degrees, focused on how we might collectively and individually harness the "enormous occult force" of sexual energy to bring the Third Term of the Trinity into being. The four degrees were, in order of rank, Priestess, Jackal of the Courtyard, Venerable Warrior, and Magnificent Invincible Knights. A newspaper, *La Flèche* (The Arrow), disseminated the group's thinking. Naglowska made no attempts to hide her notorious ideas. Madeline DeSpencer writes that,

'From the outset Maria made it abundantly clear that she would not shy away from embracing the Luciferian aspects of her overtly Satanic feminist vision. It would be impossible to divorce the Satanic elements from her philosophy which was so grounded in the unification of opposites.'

Despite her obsession with Satan (and her assertion of the importance of Judas), Naglowska maintained a respect for the Church, recognising the part they had played to date with regards to the facilitation of the progression through the apexes of the Trinity. She writes in *La Flèche* that, "We render homage to the learned men of the Church for having known how to keep a secret until the end", and that the Catholic Church "have given the world what they were supposed to give", as if to confirm that the Church were conspiratorially aware of the progression she laid out.

At the heart of her group's practices was sexual magic, or as she called it, "ritual love". The basis of this was bringing shame into the light, as she explains in *La Flèche*:

> *'the deep flesh is the root of the spirit, and the divine energy touches the man and the woman in the organs concerning which they feel shame [...] it is not the organ that is shameful, but the ill will of the humans who make use of it for themselves and not for God'.*

Naglowska foresaw that ritual sex activities would replace Mass, describing an alternative Golden Mass befitting the feminine age. In *La Flèche* Issue 6, she expounds the ritual in detail, with its separate hours dedicated to Moses ("founder of Witnessing"), Jesus ("Establisher of Sacrifice") and finally, "life liberated from the prison of the flesh". The Golden Mass culminates in ritual sexual intercourse as a form of celebration, with the direction being to "now live the Third hour, in order to understand it". A further ritual, that of The Hanging Mystery, is described in Naglowska's book, *Advanced Sex Magic: The Hanging Mystery Initiation* (2011). This act of ritual strangulation is cut short "at the exact moment when the strangulation risks becoming fatal" and ends with both the hanged man and "the woman", being left in the "cellar of executions" until dawn. In The *Light of Sex* (2011), Naglowska writes that "The Man comes away from this test shaken in his Reason, and he is then the Sublime Madman of which the secret scriptures speak". It is through these acts that Satan, in the form of the spirit of evil and darkness, is brought into the light. It is perhaps this somewhat redemptive quality that leads Donald Traxler, the contemporary translator of Naglowska's works into English, to assert that "she was not a Satanist. She was, on the other hand, a mystic, a philosopher, and a superb writer". Yet there is a venerative aspect to this redemption and purification process that Satan goes through, which renders this statement somehow defensive. For Traxler, it's as if to be taken seriously a theory and set of practices simply cannot *be* Satanic in nature. Which, in a sense, proves Naglowska's point regarding society being unready for the Third Term. Indeed, this is what Naglowska would herself proclaim. Following a vision of the Second World War, and a dream of her own impending death, she left Paris in 1936 to be with her daughter back in Switzerland. Naglowska died on the 17th April and, having named no successor, the Brotherhood disintegrated.

Madeline DeSpencer wonders whether the world is now better prepared for Maria de Naglowska's teachings:

> *'Maria may well have been correct in her assessment and the world was not ready for her mission [...] Perhaps now the world is ready for those epiphanies of the Abjected Angel, for those secrets once taught among hunted Gnostics, for those mysteries of blood and sex taught by Sabbath fires, for the masses of the Paraclete and the true power of the priestess. If we are now in that third age, may we be illuminated by the descending dove of Lucifer and her flaming star.'*

Were Naglowska's ideas to take root once again, many contemporary feminists might find her teachings in need of, at the very least, a re-work. The question of whether or not Naglowska was a feminist is a complicated question to answer. She wrote sincerely in *La Flèche* that, "women must indeed, and very soon, replace men in the higher direction of public affairs". Nevertheless gender essentialism dominates her worldview. For Naglowska, sex and gender are the same, women are only ever 'feminine', and with that comes a set of traits opposing those which belong to men (as well as accordingly delineated roles). From a queer perspective such simplistic binaries do not hold up; through failing to acknowledge that gender is a construct they exclude many women and non-binary people from liberation. As such, there can be no equality. But equality is not something that Naglowska is particularly interested in. We cannot be sure whether she is interested in women's liberation as a principle in itself. Hierarchy and exclusivity are placed centrally within her theories and practice, and references to social scale are threaded throughout *La Flèche*. For example:

> '... the man cannot progress except by uniting himself regularly with a superior woman, and the woman cannot advance along the line of perfection if she does not receive the fecundating and illuminating sperm of the man frequently enough.'

Such sentiments are framed even more explicitly in the following statement from *Initiatic Eroticism*:

> 'According to us - we insist - human beings do not in themselves present an object of interest, just as for an electrical engineer the question is not one of making all wires good, but of choosing the best for the electrical installation that he proposes. The Son must be reborn, and each one is not necessarily required for that: so much the better for those who are useful to Him, so much for those who are not'.

Certain categories of people are pushed to the sidelines in Naglowska's vision for the future. In the 2013 English version of *Initiatic Eroticism*, a footnote describes the omission from the translation of the following instruction in Naglowska's description of the Golden Mass: "you will not introduce into your midst any man of black or red color, for those races are expired." The translator, Donald Traxler, by no means endorses this, but does make a somewhat excusing assumption that Naglowska "would not have included [this instruction] today". We do not know this for sure. In Traxler's comment, and simple solution for the fact of Naglowska's racism, we bear witness to a tendency within modern occultism - and in the wider world - to whitewash and sanitise history. To gloss over important figures' dangerous thinking and innermost beliefs. When it comes to carrying problematic figures' work into the future there is a question here about whether we should, in fact, throw the baby out with the bathwater. To what extent can we adopt practices which were in fact formulated in the depths of exclusionary minds?

The case of Maria de Naglowska invites us to consider how inextricably linked magical practices are to the core of our being, and therefore to our politics. Can we ever separate our practices, politics and lives? The jury is out.

Annie Besant (1847 - 1933)
Supporter of the Bryant and May Matchgirls strike (1888)

Chapter Eleven

Annie Besant
Sceptical Seeker
(d. 1933)

Circling back through the 20th century we have brushed shoulders with numerous new religious movements and occult organisations, from Wicca and Thelema to the Hermetic Order of the Golden Dawn. Time-travelling to the turn of the century we now find ourselves deep in the era of an influential (though much criticised) international religion, which Maria de Naglowska argues in *Initiatic Eroticism*, "prostituted the divine by cutting it into small pieces of cake that are easy to digest". As we shall discover, however, Theosophy possesses a complex cosmology which synthesises Hindu philosophy with what its detractors have generally labelled Western "pseudo-science". The Theosophical Society's impact would nevertheless thread down through time, shaping all that has followed when it comes to igniting a predisposition for orientalism within the Western occult scene. This is a tale of colonialism, socialism, and the Christian-turned-occultist pipeline. This is the tale of an activist, a political fighter, an intellectual, a seemingly erratic seeker and a somewhat problematic figure. Allow me to introduce the very changeable Annie Wood Besant.

> *'Looking back to-day over my life, I see that its keynote - through all the blunders and blind mistakes, and clumsy follies - has been this longing for sacrifice to something felt as greater than the self.'* ~ Annie Besant, 1885.

Born in 1847, "within the sound of Bow Bells", Annie Wood's childhood and innermost thoughts are meticulously described in her

1885 autobiography. This invaluable resource explains how her religiosity flowered at a young age; she recalls her child self as mystical "to the very fingertips". Like many of the women we have met so far in these pages, Annie was prone to visions and vivid dreams, and attributes this disposition to her Celtic heritage. In addition to being precociously spiritual, she seems to have been a capable reader too, tackling *Paradise Lost* as a girl, of which she notes in youthful Luciferian awe that, "the devil was to me no horned and hoofed horror, but the beautiful shadowed archangel, and I always hoped that Jesus, my ideal Prince, would save him in the end."

Of upperclass parentage, Annie Besant married a clergyman - Frank Besant - in 1867. The fact that she had attempted to break the engagement, but was talked down by her mother, foreshadowed the unhappiness of the couple in years to come. Besant describes the way in which her husband found her too fiery, impassioned and willful to make a suitably obedient wife. Certainly independent, she began making her own living as a writer of short stories in 1868, though a novel she submitted to the *Family Herald* was deemed "too political" to publish. A son was born in 1869, and a daughter followed in 1870. In the wake of her daughter's birth Besant's health began to wane along with her Christian beliefs. In her autobiography, Besant recalls that her misery was so great, and her marriage so unhappy, that following an argument with her husband one day, she came very close to drinking chloroform. Doctors' attempts to revive her spirits failed. Beyond health, this was a spiritual sickness. Besant describes, "awakening to what the world was, to the facts of human misery, to the ruthless tramp of nature and of events over the human heart, making no difference between innocent and guilty." This turn prompted a growing interest in political activism - a move to rural Lincolnshire had enabled engagement with agricultural union matters. Her husband disapproved of this. Her growing political involvement, along with the renouncement of Christianity, brought the Besants' marriage to an end in 1873. In her own words,

> '... the crisis came. I was told that I must conform to the outward observances of the Church, and attend the Communion; I refused. Then came the distinct alternative; conformity or exclusion from home - in other words, hypocrisy or expulsion. I chose the latter.'

Gaining custody of her daughter, Besant returned to London, supplementing her husband's allowance by making a living first as a seamstress then as a housekeeper, all the while deepening her interests in activism and her newly discovered atheism. She began to attend South Place Chapel, the centre of Freethought in London at the time, and the forerunner to the present day's Conway Hall Ethical Society in Bloomsbury. She also joined the National Secular Society, becoming firm friends with its founder, Charles Bradlaugh. As her connections in philosophical spheres developed, Besant came to reject intuition as a basis for morals, noting in her autobiography her belief at the time that,

> '... the true basis of morality is utility; that is, the adaptation of our actions to the promotion of general welfare and happiness; the endeavour so to rule our lives that we may serve and bless mankind.'

Having started lecturing at South Place Chapel in 1875, she went on tour a month later, travelling to Birkenhead, Glasgow and Aberdeen to lecture on civil liberties, Freethought and social reform, doing what she describes as "propagandist work". Meanwhile, across the ocean at the Miracle Club in New York, the Theosophical Society was being birthed by the Spiritualist Helena Petrovna Blavatsky, her lawyer friend Colonel Henry Steel Olcott, and the estotericist William Quan Judge. Financially backed by Olcott, the Theosophical Society existed to spread the teachings of Theosophy - a new religious movement based on Blavatsky's mystical writings. These teachings, combining Eastern and Western thought, were said to have been received from the Masters of the Ancient Wisdom - a secret international fraternity of spiritual adepts, members of which had initiated Blavatsky during her alleged time in the Himalayas. According to Blavatsky, there was an ancient, universal wisdom underpinning all religions, understood and conserved by the Masters (here we see certain echoes of the Witch-Cult hypothesis, with something of a cosmic evolutionary spin). Blavatsky's "secret doctrine" was formed of the perfect synthesis of religion and science; a synthesis which has been deemed lost as humanity has unfurled through the ages. Theosophy draws ideas from Hinduism and Buddhism, such as reincarnation and karma, and was a well from which the later New Age movement would drink. Annie Besant was to find a thirst-quenching well in it too.

The editor of the *Pall Mall Gazette*, William Stead, asked Besant to review Blavatsky's book *The Secret Doctrine* (1888) in part because nobody else would touch it. By this time, as Gary Lachman points out, Besant was "a political firebrand", having been arrested for supporting birth control and heavily involved in both the Bloody Sunday and Match Girls demonstrations. The *Secret Doctrine* acted like a lightning bolt to Besant:

> *'I was dazzled, blinded by the light in which disjointed facts were seen as parts of a mighty whole, and all my puzzles, riddles, problems, seemed to disappear. The effect was partially illusory in one sense, in that they all had to be slowly unravelled later, the brain gradually assimilating that which the swift intuition had grasped as truth. But the light had been seen, and in that flash of illumination I knew that the weary search was over and the very Truth was found.'*

For someone who had previously sworn away her trust in intuition and revelation, we can imagine the surprise to herself upon having her mind and heart (yet again) altered. Besant asked for an introduction to Blavatsky shortly after reading the text, and joined the Theosophical Society on the 10th May 1889. A few months later she delivered a lecture at the Hall of Science titled 'Why I Became a Theosophist'. As someone with ardent views, this willingness to boldly forsake them for a different set of views seems rigorously shameless and brazenly honest. Rather than flighty, we find in Besant a woman of deep convictions, open-mindedly embracing idea after idea. Up until now, it is *ideas* that have led Besant, but following her conversion to Theosophy, we see a new avenue open up - that of *devotion* to her guru, Helena Blavatsky. Speaking at the 18th Annual Convention of the Theosophical Society, Besant waxes lyrical about the organisation's key figure:

> *'Her real value was that she unveiled to us the secret of the Ancient Knowledge and that she put into our hands the keys by which we might ourselves unlock the gates of the inner sanctuary, that she came to us knowing the things of The Spirit and able to explain to us how we for ourselves might follow the clues which she gave; so that those who are instructed in this Esoteric Philosophy - spoken of in modern times as the Theosophical Teachings - those who are instructed in it can turn to the Vedas, can turn to the Puranas, and there find knowledge which from the ordinary reader is hidden. Thus she acts as a great Teacher, filling the function which in ancient times was carried on between the Teacher and the disciple.'*

In 1890 Blavatsky moved into Besant's house in St John's Wood, demonstrating the women's closeness. Blavatsky died just under a year later, on the 8th May 1891; a day now marked globally by Theosophists as 'White Lotus Day'. Besant succeeded her by becoming president of the Society in 1907. Since her death, Blavatsky's views on race have rightly been heavily criticised. In the second volume of

The Secret Doctrine she lays out her theories on human evolution by offering, with examples, a list of different races as having more intellect and spiritual potential than others (notably, 'Aryans'). She even goes so far as to state her approval of many of the "lower" races "fast dying out". We must remember, when considering Besant's opinions, that such ideas are central to the thesis of the book which so radically converted her to Theosophy. Despite Besant's credentials as a social reformer, this sponsoring of bigotry is simply indefensible. Several contemporary academics have raised further issues with regards to the racist views of leading Theosophists. For example, the colonisation and appropriation of the Hindu and Buddhist religions. Julian Strube notes that,

> *'Theosophists such as Blavatsky or Henry Steel Olcott made considerable efforts to assert their own authority through claims to "occult" knowledge superior to that of their Indian interlocutors.'*

Besant has been called out for her defence of the Indian caste system, something which initially seems at odds with her campaigning for Indian independence. Chandra Lekha Singh draws attention to the fact that Besant set up a school in Benares specifically for the education of upper caste boys. Scholarships were available for the "hereditary learned caste" - *ie.* Brahmins - only. Besant argued that the caste system was synonymous with the sensible organising function at the heart of the English class system, and was integral to Hinduism. Singh explains that Besant believed such divisions to be "a sign of civilised society" and that she perhaps played a key role in the strengthening of the caste system by means of her public arguments for it.

In her later years Besant took the young Jiddu Krishnamurti under her wing. He had been "discovered" by her colleague Charles Webster Leadbeater, who fervently believed that the boy would become the 'World Teacher' - a great spiritual leader and incarnation of a high tier member of the Masters of the Ancient Wisdom. Krishnamurti *was* to become a (somewhat reluctant) spiritual leader and philosopher, in time. However, he had by this point disavowed the Theosophists, slinging off his groomed identity as the World Teacher. Nevertheless, Krishnamurti remained close with Besant until her death in 1933, having been adopted by her following a protracted legal battle with his biological father.

Following Besant's death, the English writer Aldous Huxley, plus Krishnamurti and several others, brought to life one of her educational visions on 500 acres of land in Ojai, California. Besant Hill School of Happy Valley still exists today, charging over $60,000 annually for boarders. We can only contemplate what Besant, the somewhat confused but always energetic social reformer, might make of that.

Leila Waddell (1880 - 1932)
Performing the Rites of Eleusis in London (1910)

Chapter Twelve

Leila Waddell
Rag-Time Revolutionary
(d. 1932)

On 31st May 1924, *The Sydney Morning Herald* reported on the triumphant return of one of Australia's most adored musical daughters:

> *'Miss Leila Waddell, who arrived here on Tuesday from New York, is a native of Bathurst, popular here in her girlish days as a violinist from Mr. Henri Staell's studio. After a big send-off concert the enterprising girl visited London for study under Emil Sauret, thus continuing the traditions of the French school imposed by Staell, and when funds ran low she accepted an engagement as leader of the gipsy band on the stage in the London production of "The Waltz Dream," and as soloist behind the scenes. This gave an impetus to her career in a new direction, and the classic player decided on vaudeville engagements. Accordingly, in the character of "The Ragged Gipsy" she appeared during a period of years at the Coliseum, Palladium, and other theatres, and ultimately at a high salary throughout France and Germany and other countries as far as Moscow and St. Petersburg.'*

What the newspaper failed to report is that during her time abroad the "enterprising girl" Leila Waddell had been Aleister Crowley's occult co-conspirator in London, joined an Irish-revolutionary sect in New York, and laid foundations for the future of the organised organs of Thelema. Furthermore, the newspaper omits that Leila's vaudeville appearances across Europe were organised by Crowley, who instigated the Ragged Rag-Time Girls as a way to employ his beloved after she was rendered too scandalous to work. Whilst this might sound as if Waddell was indebted to Crowley, we might in fact discover that the debt was all his to pay.

The child of Irish Potato Famine refugees, Leila Ida Bathurst Waddell was indeed popular in Australia during her "girlish days". There is very little documentation regarding her youth, but we do know that in 1908, at the age of 28, she travelled to England. Alice Gorman suggests that Waddell likely met Crowley on the bohemian circuit which frequented Café Royal in London. Crowley (1910) describes the early days of their time together thus,

> *'I happened to have a few friends in my room in the evening, among them the celebrated Australian violinist, Miss Leila Waddell. It struck me that we might pass the time by a sort of artistic dialogue; I read a piece of poetry from one of the great classics, and she replied with a piece of music suggested by my reading [...] and in the silence of the room spiritual enthusiasm took hold of us; so acutely that we were all intensely uplifted, to the point in some cases of actual ecstasy'.*

In other words, a typical night in with Crowley. The two became impassioned lovers, and Waddell joined the A∴A∴, an initiatory organisation spearheaded by Crowley. In the context of the A∴A∴, Waddell was known as Soror Agatha. To Crowley, she was Laylah. Crowley, judging by his simmering accounts, assorted poems, and verbose homages, was besotted with his new girlfriend; in his short story *The Violinist* (1910) he writes,

> *'She tore life and death asunder on her strings. Up, up soared the phoenix of her song; step by step on music's golden scaling-ladder she stormed the citadel of her Desire. The blood flushed and swelled her face beneath its sweat. Her eyes were injected with blood'.*

Despite Crowley possessing an erotic hunger for his muse, William Breeze (that friend of Marjorie Cameron) notes in his introduction to *Magick: Book 4* that Waddell never became one of Crowley's Scarlet Women because, "perhaps she lacked the characteristic gift of clairvoyance". This point is contested by many others and in recent years Waddell, captured iconically in photographs wearing ritual garb, has become the canonical image of the Scarlet Woman. Many note Waddell's collaborative role - along with Crowley and Mary D'Este - in writing *Magick*, as an example of Waddell's powers and importance. In Part III of the book, which is the culmination of a dialogue between Crowley and Waddell, a playfulness and equality is revealed through a footnote in which Waddell affectionately mocks the Great Beast:

> *'It is amusing to observe that FRATER PERDURABO [Crowley], when He had completed the series of discourses in Part II, supposed that he had exhausted the subject. Everyone (He thought) would say "Oh, that is the meaning of the Wand!" "Now I understand about the Cup!"*
>
> *It never occurred to Him that there were people who had not done Magick. He only thought that there might be a few who were doing it badly!!!!!!'*

Regardless of the power dynamic at play in their relationship, there is no doubt that Crowley was in awe of Waddell. Her musicality inspired him endlessly and her status as his muse welcomed in a very productive period in his life. This status, however, was elevated to the role of collaborator through their work together on the *Rites of Eleusis*. These rites, made up of seven parts (for seven celestial bodies), were conceived during a visit to the house of naval commander Guy Marston. Marston is perhaps most memorable for his belief that, "married English women could be induced to masturbate by the sound of tom-tom drums" (Gorman, 2019). It is fitting, then, given the group's interest in ecstatic magic, that they devised a rite involving music, poetry and dance which would enable the audience to achieve these heightened states. The *Rites of Eleusis* were born, and performed by Crowley, Waddell and the dancing poet Victor Neuburg in late 1910 at London's Caxton Hall, with tickets priced at five guineas. The performance successfully brought the burgeoning A∴A∴ into the limelight and marked what J. F. Brown terms Crowley's "first great evangelization". Whilst this may be true, the rites were not Crowley's alone and history is at risk of forgetting Thelema's true forebears. Leila Waddell is one of them.

In the wake of this double-edged publicity Waddell, as Tracy Tupman explains, struggled to find work. Crowley's formation of the Ragged Rag-Time Girls vaudeville group supplied a solution. In his autobiography Crowley writes that the women were,

> '... *badly in need of protection. Leila Waddell was the only one with a head on her shoulders. Of the other six, three were dipsomaniacs, four nymphomaniacs, two hysterically prudish, and all ineradicably convinced that outside England everyone was a robber, ravisher and assassin. They all carried revolvers, which they did not know how to use; though prepared to do so on the first person who spoke to them.*'

Despite these alleged fears, the group toured widely; beginning in London, travelling to Russia and then spending two months in Glasgow, though Crowley was increasingly absent due to O.T.O. commitments. Waddell then travelled to New York, where she sold valuable instruments for auction at the behest of an uncle in Glasgow. We find a short interview with her in the aforementioned issue of the *Sydney Morning Herald*:

"'New York is full of 'crooks,' and I was much relieved when these valuable art treasures ceased to be in my possession. While in New York I took lessons from Leopold Auer, now 79 years of age, teacher of Elmann, Heifetz, and scores of other celebrities. After the war they bought a house for their old master on Riverside Drive, furnished it, and started him with a donation of 55,000 dols. In English money he charged me five guineas merely to hear me play, and on 'passing' I had three months with him at 35 dols. a lesson. Then, after touring to earn more money, I did another three months. He has an absolute genius for teaching, and can be quite agreeable when you play so as to win his approval.'"

Once again Waddell's relationship with Crowley is obscured, as are her more radical activities.

With the advent of World War I, the most radical of Ireland's republicans saw the opportunity to push for Irish independence. This republican stance was controversial given that to be anti-English at this time could inevitably entail being pro-German. Despite this, Waddell tightly held her republican stance and joined what Gorman terms "a secret revolutionary group". Crowley arrived in the States in 1914, where he contributed to the pro-German publication *The Fatherland* - a weekly which received part of its funding from a German propaganda cabinet (Keller, 1971). We cannot know whether Waddell shared Crowley's sentiments, just as we cannot know to what extent Crowley's complicity in fascism was scandal-mongering,

In July 1915, Waddell, Crowley and several companions sailed in a motorboat down the Hudson River to the Statue of Liberty. Details of their escapades were published in the *New York Times* on the 13th July:

'The members of the party consider themselves members of the secret Revolutionary Committee of Public Safety of the Provisional

Government of the Irish Republic, and their early morning mission of July 3 was to declare the independence of the Irish Republic, which included a declaration of war against England, and to pledge their allegiance to the government of their vision. The little launch passed from the river into the bay and stopped off Bedloe's Island, under the Statue of Liberty. The time and place chosen for the ceremony were considered brightly propitious. There was the poetic significance of the dawn, the great figure of Liberty enlightening the world was symbolic of the dreamed-of republic, the season was the anniversary of the Declaration of Independence of the United States. And the leader of the party, Crowley, in whose mysticism there is something of astrology, had read the heavens and found that the conjunction of certain stars was auspicious for Ireland at exactly 4:32 o'clock on the morning of July 3. So, with the launch a few feet off Bedloe's Island, at the moment of 4:32 o'clock, Crowley rose to begin the ceremony.'

Having delivered a speech in which he declared Irish independence and war on England, tore up his British passport and unfurled the Irish flag, the newspaper continued,

'the launch headed up the Hudson River, proceeding near the western shore, Miss Waddell playing patriotic Irish airs on her violin. The music and the large Irish flag, now plainly visible in the increasing light, identified the boat to the seamen on the German ships interned at the Hoboken waterfront, and they cheered the small company of Irishmen lustily. The Captain of the Hamburg-American line tug which happened to be standing off with steam up near the Vaterland, turned out into the river and escorted the launch to its landing at Fiftieth Street. Incidentally it was noted by those in the launch that as they passed by the French and English ships at the piers on the eastern side of the river the sailors on them cheered as loudly as the Germans had. [...] The party left the launch and went to Jack's restaurant for breakfast,

where a number of late revelers did not seem to disturb the spirit of their gathering.'

Following this very public escapade Waddell toured the United States and played lunchtime concerts for migrant workers arranged by the YMCA. Gorman notes that Waddell "loved this experience and considered it the greatest work of her career". Her much-heralded return to Australia led to further teaching engagements whilst she cared for her poorly father. As far as we know, Waddell lived a peacefully scandal-free life back in her homeland before becoming gravely ill and dying of uterine cancer at the age of 52. How much or how little she continued to engage with the occult, or with her Irish republican sensibilities, remains a mystery.

Moina Mathers (1845 - 1928)
Rites of Isis Portrait by Travis Simpkins (2022)

Chapter Thirteen

Moina Mathers
A Subversive Wife
(d. 1928)

Just as Leila Waddell's story has historically been subsumed into the legend of her lover Crowley, the tale of Moina Mathers' colourful life has all but been erased due to the largesse of her husband. Samuel MacGregor Mathers was one of the three founding members of the Hermetic Order of the Golden Dawn - the occult organisation to which Pamela Colman Smith belonged. As with Colman Smith, Moina Mathers was a schooled artist of a visionary persuasion. And akin to Leila Waddell and her lover Crowley, Moina was the absolute equal of her husband Samuel. The life of Moina Mathers demonstrates how one can be both a loyal, devoted wife, whilst also subverting the traditional gender roles ascribed to both women of her time and the women of today.

Born in Geneva in February 1865, Mina Bergson was the daughter of a Polish Jew who studied piano under Chopin, and a Yorkshirewoman. According to Mary K. Greer, it was due to antisemitism that the family (including their seven children) left Geneva for Paris before settling in London. The likelihood is that their household was a multilingual and staunchly Orthodox one - Mina's brother Henri Bergson had been talent scouted for his academic achievements by the chief rabbi of Paris himself, and went on to become a famed intellectual (though Moina had little contact with Henri throughout her life). At the age of 15, Mina began her studies at the Slade art school in London, to which she was awarded a scholarship in 1883. It was there that she met her wealthy lifelong friend (and occasional foe)

Annie Horniman, of the eclectic and renowned Horniman Museum's founding family. The Slade was a progressive arts institution for its time, admitting more women than men and permitting them to attend life drawing classes rather than the traditional concession to paint and draw from sculptures and artistically rendered likenesses. Mina was not only a gifted artist but also a brave woman; upon graduation she took up residency away from her family, alone in a studio on Fitzroy Street in London's bustling West End.

From her youth, Mathers possessed a fascination with Egyptian art and symbolism, and spent hours perusing the British Museum for inspiration. It was here that she would first lock eyes with her companion-for-life, Samuel Mathers.

Greer elucidates on the encounter:

'Mathers had been searching for a partner in his magical endeavours. Mina Bergson - artistic, psychically sensitive, beautiful, from a family rooted in the Kabbalah, drawn to the ancient religious symbols housed in the museum, a Taurus to his Capricorn, ripe for his training - was perfect.'

It was in a back-room of her Fitzroy Street studio that Bergson became the first initiated member of the Hermetic Order of the Golden Dawn, having illustrated its charter shortly before. The Order decreed equality between men and women as a foundational point, Samuel Mathers having been influenced by the women's suffragist and practitioner of Christian pantheism, Anna Kingsford, who he met in 1886. Annie Horniman was initiated shortly after Mina; the two were co-conspirators, after all. Following her marriage to Samuel Mathers, Mina Bergson became Moina Mathers. Ithell Colquhoun comments on the equality of this mutual name-change; it worked both ways:

'He [Samuel Mathers] *had for some time harboured Jacobite dreams, besides the lore of ancient civilisations which always*

coloured his thought. It was he who changed her name. [...] in order to give it a more Highland sound. In her turn she called him Zan, seeing in him a resemblance to Zahoni, hero of Sir Edward Bulmer-Lytton's eponymous novel (1845).'

Following her initiation into the newly formed Hermetic Order of the Golden Dawn, Moina Mathers assumed the magical name of Vestigia, a shortened version of her magical motto, *Vestigia Nulla Retrorsum*, one translation of which is "no tracks turned back". Certainly very few tracks would be left for historians: there are only brief reminiscences of Mathers' recorded life to piece together into a whole. We do know, however, that after their marriage Moina and Samuel took up residence on the Horniman estate, where regular time was given over to what Greer terms "metaphysical salons and evenings of psychic experimentation". Mathers proved to be gifted as a clairvoyant and in the techniques of scrying, transmitting her knowledge down through the years in the 'Flying Rolls' of the Golden Dawn. These were missives from the leadership, offering guidance in both thought and magical technique. Mathers is the author of several, as was her husband. These rare written offerings enable us to glean insights into Moina's practices and beliefs. For example, in Flying Roll XXI (titled *Know Thyself*) she writes:

> *'It will be best, then, for us to live amongst our fellows, and in our contact with them we are advised to avoid preaching and proselytising; which often leads also to a condition of self righteousness in the Preacher, and is generally useless to the listener.*
>
> *Rather would we influence them by our example, and by keeping our thoughts as well as our actions pure.'*

It is hard to avoid a comparison with the evangelising of Annie Besant here. For members of the Golden Dawn secrecy was key, and as Denis Denisoff (2022) writes, they had a "precept of ritual not as a worship of a particular goddess or god, but as a private, consecrated act of extension through another realm". This privacy, and what Mathers describes as "purity", go hand in hand. The marriage of Moina and Samuel Mathers was a celibate one, with Moina, as Colquhoun suggests, valuing her virginity. Despite her personal disinterest in sexual intercourse, Moina Mathers retained a non-judgemental approach, careful never to press her values and notions onto anyone else. In terms of sex and sexuality, the Golden Dawn was progressive in a passive rather than a pushy way. To be a celibate woman at this point in time was to be an independent woman within the context and contract of marriage. The fact that Collquhoun suggests that Mathers' celibacy must be a sign of hidden childhood sexual abuse is testament to the power and strangeness of a woman saying "no".

During their early years setting up house in Paris, the couple's passion for Egyptian art and spirituality, along with a drive to encourage a new spiritual community with an interest in Egypt, moved them to perform *The Rites of Isis* at Théâtre La Bodinière. Such a move was a clear shift from the pair's preference for secrecy with regards to ritual. But just as Samuel had been compelled to move their home from London to Paris based on a psychic message from one of the Golden Dawn's Secret Chiefs (not unlike the Masters we have met in previous chapters), Moina too received permission for the performance from the goddess Isis herself. Denisoff (2014) quotes the journalist André Gaucher's description of events:

> *'The women and men, dressed in multi-coloured, neo-Greek robes, performed simple ceremonial rites involving lighting a cauldron of perfume and either burning flowers and sheaves of wheat in a cauldron or simply tossing them. [...] the worshippers prostrated themselves and shouted "Isis! Isis! Isis".'*

Denisoff (2022) praises the "feminist resonance" of the performance. This is echoed in an interview Frederic Lees conducted with Moina in 1900:

MOINA MATHERS: A SUBVERSIVE WIFE

'when a religion symbolises the universe by a Divine Being, is it not illogical to omit woman, who is the principal half of it, since she is the principal creator of the other half - that is, man?'

For Moina and Samuel Mathers, beliefs and actions travelled hand in hand. Their ethics and morals (without moralising) came to the fore during the war years. The couple opened the doors of their house for the recruitment and training of hundreds of British and American soldiers in France. It is understandable that during this period their magical practices took something of a back seat. By this point Samuel had been expelled from the Order anyway, in part because the rest of the leadership disagreed with his plan to promote Aleister Crowley up the ranks. The Order was imploding, and scandals were rife. Members who remained loyal to Mathers followed his leadership into the splinter group Alpha et Omega. When Samuel died of the Spanish flu in 1918, Moina, along with J. W. Brodie-Innes, took control of this splinter organisation, guiding it with firm hands.

Mathers soon ran into friction with one of Alpha et Omega's members - Violet Firth (later known as Dion Fortune) - who she expelled for spilling organisational secrets in Firth's recently published book. Owen argues that Mathers' attitude was somewhat to blame, stating that she "proved as temperamental and autocratic as her husband had been." In light of Fortune's response, it's hard not to side with Mathers, however: Fortune later implicitly accused Mathers for not only psychically attacking her, but also for murdering a fellow occultist, Netto Fornario, who had in fact died 18 months *after* Moina passed away in 1928. Fortune describes the alleged psychic attack on herself in detail in her book, *Psychic Self Defence*:

'I experienced the sensation of being whirled through the air and falling from a great height and found myself back in my body. But my body was not where I had left it, but in a heap in the far corner of the room, which looked as if it had been bombed.'

Unlike Mathers, Fortune was full of exclusionary judgements and proselytising; perhaps revealing why her name, and not Mathers', has endured in the occult halls of fame. According to Fortune, abortion is an abomination, homosexuals and those suffering from "frigidity" must be excluded from rites, and "the more important parts in some rituals are best done by tall and powerfully built men" (1930b). Given these views, and Mathers' seeming open-mindedness, it's unsurprising that the two were at odds.

The grieving Moina Mathers' assertive leadership in the case of Fortune is a far cry from the meek attitude that she is ascribed to her by Greer, who writes that she

> 'epitomises the Victim [...] She has an inner monster who is the dogmatic widow. We do not want to be reminded of the Victim's vulnerability - how she appears weak and fragile within a hierarchical relationship in which her quiescence signifies her "service" - in Moina's case it was service to MacGregor [Mathers] and the Golden Dawn'.

To the contrary, there are no signifiers that Moina was the victim of her husband's power. Unlike many women of her time, she was relieved of child rearing duties and able to focus on her passions - magic (specifically clairvoyance) and art. She designed and decorated Golden Dawn literature, along with adorning their beautiful, atmospheric temples. She was able to pursue her dreams of making art, earning self knowledge and seeking knowledge of the Divine. She lived quietly but influentially. She was a devoted wife and a feminist, proving that even in magical spheres, the two need not always be mutually exclusive.

Sojourner Truth (1797- 1883)
Sculpture in Battle Creek by Tina Allen

Chapter Fourteen

Sojourner Truth
Power in Forgiveness
(d. 1883)

'Where did your Christ come from? From God and a woman! Man had nothin' to do wid Him.' (Sojourner Truth, 1851).

In May 1851, the Ohio Woman's Rights Convention was held at Stone Church, Akron. In uttering the above words, Sojourner Truth cemented her place in history as an early - and certainly intersectional - warrior against the oppression of women. Frances D. Gage describes the atmosphere surrounding Truth's speech that day:

'I have never in my life seen anything like the magical influence that subdued the mobbish spirit of the day, and turned the sneers and jeers of an excited crowd into notes of respect and admiration. Hundreds rushed up to shake hands with her...'

Sojourner Truth was a mystic, an abolitionist, a woman of colour, a Spiritualist and a gifted orator. She was anti-capital punishment and pro-health reform. She was a former slave who fought vehemently for the liberation of herself, her children and others. She endured hardships that are barely imaginable, and broke down barriers that were, at the time, often insurmountably beyond the awareness of elites and the poor alike. She was immensely funny and deeply brave. She fought for radical change with fierceness and humility. And perhaps most of all, she was a great believer in the friendship and inclusive forgiveness of Christ. Living her beliefs - acting on them with grace and bravery - is her greatest legacy of all.

Let us wind the time machine back to the late 1790s, New York State. Do you recall the Hudson River, where Leila Waddell and her lover Crowley declared Irish independence? We find ourselves seven miles west of that same river now, in Ulster County. A child named Isabella is born to two slaves - James and Elizabeth - who are under the ownership of Colonel Johannis Hardenbergh. Though the large family (of which Isabella is the youngest child) have been granted a cottage and some land, they lose all rights to this upon the death of Hardenbergh. Instead they live with many other slaves in a damp basement where disease and illness are rife. Sinking under the weight of a thoroughly understandable depression, James and Elizabeth are brought to their knees as their children, one by one, are sold off and separated from them. At the age of nine, Isabella is sold to an English family for $100 and the story of her slavery - and eventual liberation - begins in earnest.

Following this initial sale, into a family who beat her until blood was drawn and lifelong scars formed, Isabella was sold on again, and once again, until she became the slave of the Dumont family, in whose service she spent 16 years being subjected to the most vile physical (and sometimes sexual) abuse. Like many slaves, Isabella developed an incongruous attachment to her keeper, believing him to be a God of sorts, as her biographer Nell Irvin Painter explains:

> 'She had believed that submission to Dumont was the same as being true to God, a reasoning that also prevailed among slave owning southerners with regard to their children as well as their slaves.'

In today's psychological language we might class Isabella's attachment to the Dumonts as "disorganised" in style: a confusing fear and hatred blurred and prevaricatingly wrapped up in unwarranted love.

Whilst indentured to the Dumonts, Isabella married a fellow slave by the name of Thomas and gave birth to five children. It was with one of her children - baby Sophia - that she snuck out the door, a handkerchief of supplies in her grip, and found her way with the help of a friend to the house of an abolitionist couple who bought her and her baby from the Dumonts at $25 for a year. This set her on the path towards legal freedom, which she eventually won in 1827. Her other children, however, were yet to find liberation. Isabella discovered that her son Peter had been sold multiple times, ending up enslaved thousands of miles away in Alabama. Bolstered by her own liberation and the plotting of it, Isabella mounted a legal challenge and eventually Peter was returned to her, though he was much altered. Peter had been appallingly treated and badly beaten during his time away, and initially failed to recognise his own mother, cowering away from her embrace. Painter describes how Isabella "sought vengeance in witchcraft", calling upon her God in order to curse Peter's captors; "to "render unto them double" for what they had done to Peter". A perfectly understandable undertaking indeed.

Despite this rare act of cursing, at this time Isabella was a staunch Methodist living a temperate and simple life inspired by the doctrine of Christian perfection and willed onwards by a desire for universal love and union with God. A move to New York led to her involvement with a new religious movement founded by Matthias the Prophet (a carpenter formerly known as Robert Matthews) and supported by several wealthy businessmen. Paul E. Johnson and Sean Wilentz sum up the religious fervour of the times thus:

> *'Young women conversed with the dead, male and female perfectionists wielded the spiritual powers of the Apostles; farmers and factory hands spoke directly to God; and the heavens opened up to reveal new cosmologies to poor and uneducated Americans like Matthias...'*

Isabella left her work in service to join The Kingdom - a settlement founded by Matthias in Sing Sing village - where she would become her new patriarch's greatest ally. The Kingdom, alas, descended into chaotic adultery, bed-hopping at the behest of Matthias, financial misdemeanours and sensationalist stories in the most dreg-like annals of the penny press. Matthias was accused of murdering his devout follower and patron, Elijah Pierson, and Isabella stood by his side acting in defence and ensuring that money flowed towards his cause. Matthias was acquitted in 1835, though was then imprisoned for four months after assaulting his own daughter.

Once again, Isabella had found herself at the mercy, and occasionally the backhanded slap, of a brutal patriarch. What's more, she had publicly been branded Matthias' accomplice in the alleged poisoning of Pierson. Despite this, it was she who accompanied Matthias on his triumphant return to the outside world upon his release from prison. She also maintained her position as his disciple, finding strength in launching a slander lawsuit against her own accuser, Benjamin Folger. Despite her continued faith in Matthias' interpretation of the Biblical scriptures, the pair eventually parted ways. Johnson and Wilentz suggest that Isabella had been shaken by The Kingdom's sexual escapades, though given the wild and twisted nature of events it's likely that she, at the very least, just needed a break. Matthias had called himself the Spirit of Truth, and it was Truth that Isabella adopted as her new surname upon leaving New York. Her first name, of course, became Sojourner. And so Sojourner Truth headed eastwards, rather aptly, on Pentecost of 1843. For a devotee and seeker of the Holy Spirit, it's unsurprising that Sojourner Truth set out on the next leg of her journey on the day which marks the descent of the Holy Spirit upon the followers of Jesus Christ.

Truth found a new home in Northampton, Massachusetts, where she joined a community of like minded individuals called The Northampton Association of Education and Industry. Prominent abolitionists gave lectures there and the atmosphere was one of burgeoning gender-equality, temperance, vegetarianism and spiritual contemplation. The community aimed to be self-sustaining - originally profiting from manufacturing silk - but a focus on their religious endeavours led to financial disintegration, and the group disbanded in 1846. Around this time Sojourner Truth began dictating her autobiography to Olive Gilbert - a project which would take three years to reach completion. Truth went on to self-distribute and sell copies of *The Narrative of Sojourner Truth* for 25 cents each, using the money to pay off a mortgage on her first independent home on Park Street in Florence, Northampton. By the time of the book's publication Truth had become a regular speaker on the anti-slavery circuit, having given her first speech on the subject in May 1845, at the annual meeting of the American Anti-Slavery Society in New York City. She addressed a large women's rights meeting in 1850, which Painter terms "the first such meeting of national scope in the United States". Truth told the story of her experiences as a tortured and beaten slave in her renowned (likely Dutch) accent. She spoke not only convincingly, but with great wit and gift for timing. Painter writes that:

> *'To capture and hold her audience, she communicated her meaning on several different levels at once, accompanying sharp comments with nonverbal messages: winks and smiles provoking the "laughter" so often reported.'*

A tour followed, and she used the money earned to pay off the debts she had amassed with her autobiography's printer. According to Margaret Washington, Truth called herself an anti-slavery "apostle"; an interesting nod to Matthias' similarly apostolic impression of himself.

Working with the spirits of the dead had been commonplace at The Kingdom, but it was only later that Sojourner Truth came to fully embrace the practice of Spiritualism. Although often construed as simply a way of providing scientific proof for life after death, Anne Braude explains that Spiritualism also offered hope that in that afterlife, new freedoms might be won which were impossible to achieve in this life. Truth maintained that it was a practice, rather than a faith: Washington quotes her as responding to a question regarding whether she had "joined" the Spiritualists with the retort, "Why child, there's nothing to join." For Truth, a love of Christ and her taste for Spiritualism went hand in hand. Braude notes this as a common thread in Spiritualist circles at the time, stating that "Spiritualism's proof of God's unwillingness to sever families at death supported the new theology emerging at mid-century based on the love of Christ rather than the wrath of God."

The practices of Spiritualism - mediumship in particular - affected Truth so deeply that she left her hard-earned home in Northampton, taking her daughters to Harmonia, a utopian Spiritualist community in Michigan. Now a ghost village, Harmonia was located in Battle Creek - once a centre of the Spiritualist movement. By 1860, Truth had left Harmonia and bought land nearby, where she lived peacefully with her daughters. She gave her last major lecture in 1881, against the Wykoff Hanging Bill, and retired into the care of her children. Her last audible words, according to Margaret Washington, were spoken to a newspaper correspondent: "be a follower of Jesus", she whispered.

Truth left behind her autobiography so that we might understand not only her story but the story of slavery in America and the case for abolition. Nevertheless, the strength of her belief in forgiveness and the complex issues of justice which this gives rise to have tragically stunted the book's longevity, with Painter writing that "the *Narrative of Sojourner Truth* remains outside the canon of ex-slavery narratives. It ends, not with indictment, but with the Christian forgiveness of a slaveholder." Such forgiveness is near-impossible to comprehend in the face of colonial barbarism. Yet Truth chooses to end her biography full-circle with the conversion of her former master Dumont to the anti-slavery cause. It is as if, after everything that has befallen her, and everything that she has achieved, *this* is the crux of matters. Truth lives the lesson that, for Spiritualists, everyone is born with goodness in their hearts. The final sentence in *The Narrative of Sojourner Truth* reads, "Poor old man, may the Lord bless him, and all slave-holders partake of his spirit!" If ever a person lived her life through the lens of Jesus Christ's teachings, modelling his capacity for loving kindness and forgiveness, it was Sojourner Truth.

Marie Laveau (1801-1881)
Portrait with a snake by Jared Osterhold
Courtesy of the Osterhold Studio & Gallery

Chapter Fifteen

Marie Laveau
Voodoo Queen of New Orleans
(d. 1881)

When it comes to the subject of Marie Laveau, the most prominent Voodoo Queen of New Orleans, we find ourselves moving into deep history where scraps of yellowed newspaper in museum archives and titbits of oral history combine to form an incomplete melange of images, conversations and impressions. Oil paintings of Laveau float around in the public domain but are they truly her likeness, that of a daughter of the same name, or portraits of another woman of colour wearing Laveau's trademark *tignon*? The latter possibility draws attention to the racial stereotyping at play even in our remembrances of this singular figure. The story which lies ahead is full of holes, assumptions and guesses. Laveau's is a patchy history awash with contradictions and a good dose of fantasy on the part of her admirers and devotees. Unlike the written records we have documenting Sojourner Truth's life, not to mention her autobiography, few such threads exist when it comes to her contemporary in the Deep South. There is doubtlessly much magic and mystery at play, and when those are our ingredients, we find ourselves prone to disregarding the less savoury aspects of a tale. In the case of Laveau, the unsavoury aspects leave a bitter taste, and inevitably send us on a search for explanations.

Let us begin in New Orleans, 1801. French and Spanish colonisation has drawn to an end and American control has begun. A new regime for a new era, in which the Protestantism embraced by Sojourner Truth rules - along with money - and slavery remains disgustingly commonplace. This would be the case for the entirety of Laveau's life. Ina Johanna Fandrich writes that the chief enemy of our Voodoo Queen is not the threat of magical rivals but rather:

> *'the encroaching racism, sexism, and cultural imperialism by the strictly segregated, profit-oriented, Protestant, Anglo American new rulers of the city who violently cracked down on New Orleans' influential and predominantly female free people of colour'.*

Indeed, Laveau herself was a free woman of colour. Her mother, Marguerite, had been a slave valued at 800 pesos and was eventually sold to a man named Françoise Langlois who gave her freedom. There is much debate surrounding the question of Laveau's father, but Carolyn Morrow Long proposes that Charles Laveaux was a "prosperous free man of color who traded in real estate and slaves and owned several businesses", and that father and daughter remained close throughout their lives. Other accounts tell us that Laveau's paternal ethnicity was white French, and her father a politician. Regardless of the facts, we do know that Laveau was mixed race, and above all, Louisiana Creole.

Historical church records show that Maria Laveau married Jacques Paris at St Louis Cathedral on 27th July 1819, and according to St Louis' baptismal records they bore two children who likely died in childhood. Long notes that Jacques Paris then disappears from records, prompting wild theories of his disappearance, possession and perhaps even his transformation into a zombie. Laveau later began a relationship with Christophe Glapion, who she stayed with until his death in 1855. The couple had many children and the fact that Laveau seems to have abstained from further relationships suggests that their union was a meaningful one and his death, which occurred during the fifth decade of Laveau's life, made a significant impact. Whether it was a happy marriage is another question, and one for which there will likely remain no answers.

Working as a hairdresser, it has been suggested that Laveau used her position to glean information from her wealthy white patrons. She would allegedly use this information in the court cases she attended, fighting for the rights of the accused. Other allegations include that she was engaged in acts of blackmail and used her access to high society gossip to prop up her reputation as a Voodoo seer and conjurer. In any case, Laveau's words held great sway in the city. Long states that:

> *The Laveau legend tells us that Marie was not only beautiful and charismatic, she was shrewd, powerful, and rich. It is said that through blackmail she exercised control over the white elite and that city officials, the police, the sheriff, and the courts acquiesced to her in everything.'*

In particular, Laveau's work in prison ministry is much discussed - she fought tirelessly for the freedom of imprisoned slaves, offering pastoral care, and perhaps, in one case, administering euthanasia by means of poisoned gumbo. An article from New Orleans' *Daily Picaynne* on May 10th, 1871 describes one of Laveau's prison visits in detail:

> *'she proceeded at once to prepare an altar for the worship of the men who have been sentenced to expiate the guilt of murder on the scaffold. It consists of a box of about three feet square; above this are three pyramidal boxes, rising to a small apex on which is placed a small figure of the Virgin.*
>
> *The entire altar is draped in white; on each end of the shelving is a vase of green and white artificial flowers, and beside these a smaller vase of pink and white camellias. In the center rests a prayer book in Spanish, and framed in gold, leaning against the altar are hung saints' pictures around the walls of the*

cell. Before the altar is drawn a curtain of white muslin, deeply fringed in silver filigree. The aspect of the altar is singularly beautiful and simple.'

This insight into Voodoo practice confirms the way in which the religion is a successful and seamless fusion of Catholicism and folk magic practices. New Orleans Voodoo, in the sense of being a diasporic melting pot of African religious flavours and New World spirituality, has some crossovers with the Haitian Vodou of Maya Deren, but as Long notes, its pantheon of deities differs. Martha Ward suggests that Laveau was possibly trained by Sanité Dédé, the first Voodoo Queen of New Orleans, and a slave who had bought her way to freedom. At the same time, Ward writes of initiations that one "did not join a society like Voodoo; one sought and suffered intense initiations at the hands of the spirits. They alone chose who was worthy."

New Orleans Voodoo was a religion dominated by women of colour, though many congregation members were white. In this sense segregation was loosened somewhat within Voodoo circles. As a leader standing for abolition and justice, Laveau excelled. Fandrich writes of how she:

'represented the African heritage defiantly surviving the hegemonic strategies of a white-supremacist culture; she functioned as an assertion of female power in a patriarchal society; and she embodied outrage over the unjust distribution of power, wealth, and privilege in a profoundly class-stratified environment'.

Nevertheless, Laveau and Glapion were themselves involved in trading slaves, and the couple were recorded as buying and selling eight people of colour, though Laveau ceased trading in the wake of Glapion's death. These activities certainly form a dark blot on Laveau's character, though there is word that the whole matter of trading slaves was, for Laveau and Glapion, a front serving to hide their true activities in the realm of liberation work. Denise Alvarado describes one theory of this type, in which the pair's home served as a station on the Underground Railroad; a network of safe houses for enslaved individuals to pass through on their way to free states and countries such as Canada. This network was a dangerous one to be involved in - the Fugitive Slave Act of 1850 ensured that both escapees and their harbourers would be punished. Whilst this theory regarding the Laveau home might seem like a tenuous attempt to explain and excuse the couple's slave trading activities, there is some proof to back it up. An account by Charles Raphael, a contemporary of Laveau, describes how she had upon her working altar a statue of St. Maroon, patron saint of runaway slaves. As it was typical for stations on the Underground Railroad to communicate their status by using covert visual clues, this evidence is worth paying attention to, though it remains the sole evidence in existence.

Laveau died peacefully at her cottage in New Orleans at the age of 79. Her resting place is uncertain, though tourists and present-day devotees typically visit the Glapion crypt in St. Louis Cemetery No.1 to pay their respects and seek some of that Laveau magic. Alvarado cites a story which circulates in New Orleans, telling of how Laveau's family had her body moved to the Wishing Vault in St. Louis Cemetery No.2 in order to escape the attention of travelling visitors. And in droves, the visitors come to the Glapion tomb. It has become a tradition to mark her stone with three crossmarks whilst petitioning Laveau's spirit. Whilst some decry this as an act of vandalism others such as Alvarado point out that there is a Haitian Vodou practice named *kwasiyen* - the act of signing with a cross in order to make contact with the departed. An equally vast number of visitors attend the International Shrine of Marie Laveau at the New Orleans Healing Centre, though this was only recently erected.

The influence of Marie Laveau on New Orleans and Creole Voodoo has been potent and expansive. She has come to stand for magic as a means of liberation and the vehicle of political activism. She incorporated Catholic charity into her practice and supported those whom others had abandoned. An upstanding Christian and a powerful folk magician; the two, she proved, can both be true. The Virgin Mary and Voodoo talismans such as *gris-gris* occupied the same space upon her altars: she was Creole until her end. Nowadays the New Orleans tourist industry feasts on the ghost of Marie Laveau. As well as official tours of her grave and visits to her childhood home, it's possible to spend plenty of dollars at the occult shop *Marie Laveau House of Voodoo,* located on the jangling neon lit strip of Bourbon Street. Marie herself was an entrepreneur. Perhaps she would approve of such ventures.

Biddy Early (1798-1874)

Chapter Sixteen

Biddy Early
Medicine Woman
(d. 1874)

Let us whirl across the wild ocean now, to late 18th century Ireland where, amidst the bogs, pastures and mountain lands of Kilbarron, the cottage of a wise old woman by the name of Biddy Early lies. She is old, in bed and dying, though it shall be a peaceful death. Father Connellan, the parish priest, administers the last rites and then suddenly in the room there appears a crow. Biddy asks - or perhaps challenges - the priest to usher the crow out of the window. Father Connellan prays and prays and prays, urging God to rid the room of its imposter. Alas, the good Father has no luck this time. Biddy shakes her head, sighs, and draws a small bottle formed of blue crystal from beneath the bed sheets. She points the opening of the bottle at the crow and there! It flies out of the window.

Biddy's oft cited claim that priests have the same powers as she does, but that they're afraid to use them, rings true once again. Even here, on her deathbed, she succeeds in making a fool of the magical aspects of the Church. Adding insult to injury, she offers the blue bottle to Father Connellan, stating, as reported by folklorist Eddie Lenihan, "There 'tis for you now, an' you'll have the same powers as I had". Upon leaving the house the priest forthrightly strides to Lake Killbarron and throws the bottle, with as much force as he can muster, into its watery depths. In doing so he reveals his fear, his terror, in the face of these powers which he inevitably associates with the Devil himself because they are so utterly beyond his comprehension. Biddy dies a few hours later, though she is held firmly in the minds of those who, even today, scour Lake Kilbarron for shards of her bottle. As of 1990,

Lenihan tells us that fifteen bottles had been recovered, but none yet have proven to be Biddy's magical vessel.

Due to the fact that so much of our history has been written by erudite men of the upper classes, the lives of women like Biddy have been all but erased. As with the more bombastic figure of Marie Laveau, when it comes to the story of Biddy Early oral history truly comes into its own. Almost all that we know of Biddy Early comes from second-hand accounts drawn (and often cunningly coaxed) from the lips of the grandchildren of those who knew her, by skilled collectors of folk stories such as Lenihan, and earlier by Lady Augusta Gregory.

By all accounts Early presented herself as an unassuming woman; a good and generous neighbour, and one who would readily defend the benevolence of her peculiar skills. T. K. Long, writing in the 1990s, recounts something that Early had once told his grandfather:

'... I'm not a Witch. My cures are done by herbs and in the name of the Father, the Son and the Holy Spirit. I chat with the fairies, the good ones, the souls of the dead maybe, or angels, but never with bad ones.'

Rather than being a recluse - as wise women so often are in fairy tales - Early seems to have enjoyed raucous nights at home drinking whiskey and poteen until the early hours. Speaking to Lenihan, a man named Joe Murphy recalls that, "Twas the greatest house of all for drink. There was no pub as good as it for the local crowd that had the pluck to go there." The drink shared so readily by Early was the currency she traded in - folks came from far and wide seeking her skills in seership or herbal medicine, and paid her fee not in money but in whiskey, or bread, or bacon. There are rumours that she would take a shilling, but never more. In these terms, her lack of greed was renowned. As to the nature of her character, we cannot know because, as Lenihan notes, there has been a general resistance to speaking of her in such terms. We can certainly attribute this silence to caution regarding her ongoing "knowing", even in death.

Biddy Early's magic - of prophecy and herbal healing - was often attributed to the power of the blue bottle in her possession. Some said that there was a little man in there (Lenihan draws parallels with the story of Aladdin and his lamp), whilst others told stories of how the bottle was borrowed from the fae. Indeed, stories of how Early came across the bottle abound. One common story, recounted by Lenihan, is that Early's husband (she is rumoured to have had many) had died, leaving her penniless and unable to pay her rent, and she expected to be turned out of her home with immediate effect. Whilst out collecting sticks for her fire, a vision of her dead husband Tom appeared before her, gave her the bottle and told her that she'd be able to see the future and have enormous powers, so long as she took no money whatsoever in exchange for her healing gifts. Arriving home, Early saw inside the bottle an image of the police coming to her house, and she vowed to stop them in their tracks. Once again Tom appeared to her, and told her how to stick her adversaries stock still in the road for as long as she liked. She did just that, and the police were unable to move. She told them that she would unstick them, but that she would do the same again if they ever sought to trouble her in the future. Playing games with those in power - namely Catholic clergymen and the police - was part of Early's charm. For the most part, it was the powerless who she helped to heal, or delivered prophesies to her by means of her all-seeing bottle. Though typically in tellings of her escapades she does not deal in money, there are always prices to pay, sometimes to comical effect.

A naughtily gleeful tale is the story of the blackthorn bowel movement. The space around a well, which was likely sacred (as so many wells are), was cleared of so-called weeds and blackthorn by a local man who thought he was doing some good. Following his work, he experienced the most horrific pains in his abdomen and friends advised him to seek the help of Biddy Early. Early told him to stay away from the well, as he had likely displeased the fairies or water spirits dwelling there. She also told him, according to Lenihan, to "have a look out" for bowel movements. Sure enough, upon his next bowel movement the excretion bore a length of blackthorn. No wonder the man had been in agony!

Lenihan identifies, in these second-hand threads and snippets, the fact that in order to be healed, one must make an inner deal and place their trust in both Biddy Early and the cure:

'In general it may be said that in the whole matter of cures there were basically two choices. First choice was Biddy's - to cure or not. Second choice was the sufferer's - to be cured or not.'

Having decided to accept a cure, and having been offered one by Early, it was vitally important to follow the wise woman's instructions to the letter, lest the cure be thwarted. Such is the case in a story that Bridget Dinan tells Lenihan, in which a bedridden man whose wife fails to administer the cure in the exact manner told to her by Early, remains bedridden for life. Nevertheless, the thwarted cure has an unexpected effect: the man is able to just "tell things", such as if someone had died three miles away, without having any recourse to knowledge of such an event.

Early's gift of knowledge - *fios feasaithe* - deeply troubled the clergymen who had the bizarre fortune to share a parish with her. Her otherworldly powers seemed to contradict or undermine their own, and the rattling effect of this led them to suspect dark dealings and pacts with unsavoury forces. As we have seen, Early made no attempts to hide her activities from the Church. Nevertheless, for the large part she seems to have defended herself against accusations. There is evidence, however, that she appeared in Ennis court in 1865, charged under the 1586 Witchcraft Statute. The trial was possibly thrown out due to lack of evidence, suggesting the support of locals for her cause (or their fear around testifying). Either way, as we know (and according to what is likely her birth certificate), she died peacefully in her own bed nine years later. Speaking of Early's relationship with the Church, Mr. Fahy, in conversation with Lady Augusta Gregory, states that,

> 'The priests were against her; often Father Boyle would speak of her in his sermons. They can all do those cures themselves, but that's a thing it's not right to be talking about.' This theme - of priests having powers but failing to use them, or hiding their possibility, is present throughout recollections of Early's powers, and mirrors her own statement about clergymen being "afraid to use them.'

Another example appears in a tale told to Gregory by Daniel Shea:

> 'The priests don't do cures by the same means, and they don't like to do them at all. It was in my house that you see that Father Gregan did one on Mr. Phayre. And he cured a girl up in the mountains after, and where is he now but in a madhouse. They are afraid of the power they do them by, that it will be too strong for them. Some say the bishops don't like them to do cures because the whiskey they drink to give them courage before they do them is very apt to make drunkards of them.'

The notion that priests have magical healing powers, but are afraid to use them, is prominent in reminiscences of Biddy Early. Whether or not it is true, it certainly must have been something of a comfort to the god-fearing locals and travellers who visited Early for assistance: if their clergymen had special powers that were of a good nature, surely the powers belonging to Early couldn't be those of the Devil. Though Early's healing powers were typically used for good works, especially for the poor whom she lived amongst, John Rainsford notes that there are stories of her use of "transference" - the passing of an ailment from human to animal - which undercut Lenihan's insistence of her kindly treatment of animals. With regards to these contradictions the best we can do is to get mathematical, and note which side accrues the greatest number of recollections and accounts. On this front, Lenihan wins hands down; his research is vast and thorough.

Following her death, Early's community-oriented healing powers moved from the realm of local gossip to legendary international status. A section on her work in Lady Gregory's 1920 volume *Visions and Beliefs in the West of Ireland* made public a large number of recollections of Early, which laid the groundwork for her becoming a household name; such was the intriguing nature of the tales recollected. Twenty years after Biddy Early died, Lady Gregory took her poorly friend, the poet W. B. Yeats (also the friend of Pamela Colman Smith), for restorative walks around the area where Early had lived. Walking on this land had a curative effect on the writer and, according to Holly May Walker-Dunseith, Yeats thanked it for mending his nervous ailment. Perhaps Early's healing influence lived on in the hills she so often wandered amongst in order to restock her undoubtedly jam-packed cabinet of herbs, with which she only seems to have conducted very good and fair works indeed.

Isobel Gowdie (~1632, n.d.)
Isobel Gowdie Encounters a Demon
Painting by Ian Howard RSA

Chapter Seventeen

Isobel Gowdie
The Confessor
(d. date unknown)

𝕴n the mid-1600s, a Scottish Highland farmer's wife by the name of Isobel Gowdie was walking nearby the town of Drumduan when she met the Devil for the first time. Whatever her emotional experience of this surely terrifying occurrence, she "covenanted with him" and made a pact to meet him at night time in the church of Auldearn, east of the River Nairn. She kept her promise, and there he was, standing at the reader's desk with a great black book in his hand. She stood before him and "renuncet Jesus Christ and my baptisme", then took the witches' stance (a hand on her skull and the other underfoot). In a vampiric motion, the devil puckered his lips and sucked blood from Isobel's shoulder, forming a mark. The devil spat Isobel's blood into his hand and trickled it onto her head, saying, "I baptise thee Janet, in my own name".

The demonic pair met again, and then on their third meeting Isobel Gowdie engaged in sexual intercourse with this rough man, whose genital attributes she described in erotic detail to a court in Auldearn in 1662. The court was composed of the village minister, Harry Forbes, the sheriff deputy, William Dallas, and nine witnesses. We are in the midst of the Scottish witch trials and Isobel will likely be strangled and burned for her confessions. The question we ask ourselves in this chapter is, was Isobel ill with madness, or was she in fact the witch she so readily claimed to be? Did she truly wander into fairy hills and copulate with the Devil? Did she kill others at will using magical means? Or was she unstable, playing to her audience, perhaps suffering from ergotism as a result of ingesting infected grains? Above all, which of these conclusions are fantastical and which are plausible? And is the fantastical, in fact, entirely plausible?

As historian P.G. Maxwell-Stuart writes, the Scottish Highlands were in turmoil at this time; occupied by English troops bent on dismantling a long-held way of life, and a Protestant *Kirk* (Church) riddled with an administration desperately scrabbling around for favour within the new order of things. Chaos reigned. Maxwell-Stuart deftly describes the situation:

> *'We have, then, a country with a distinctive but fissiparous religious tradition invaded by another; an alien civil and legal tradition imposed, with greater or lesser efficiency, by force; armed resistance by parts of the country with a quite different set of traditions from the rest; an invader with constant problems of his own; and the outbreak of what looks like a series of atrocities [...] This is the background to the apparent swell of witchcraft which broke out into what seemed to be a period of more intensive prosecution than Scotland had known before...'*

Whilst many of those accused of witchcraft during this period had their confessions tortured out of them, Isobel Gowdie seems to have offered up her experiences willingly and with pride; there is no evidence of exceptional maltreatment in her case (though she was most likely held in solitary confinement for the duration of her trial). Instead, her confessions have an almost ecstatic quality to them: lascivious, orgiastic, granular in detail and magical to the core. Many historians, such as Maxwell-Stuart and Emma Wilby, make note that the themes at play in Gowdie's confessions are not uncommon to other confessions made at the time (demonic copulation and vampiric devils aside). What truly stands out in Gowdie's confessions, of which there were four, is the intense level of detail and the fervency of expression. Of Gowdie's claim that frogs were yoked onto a plough, Maxwell-Stewart writes that, "this is the kind of thing one expects from a poet, and reminds one of nothing so much as the Queen Mab speech in *Romeo and Juliet*". Meanwhile Wilby draws upon the experience of the confessions' readers, who might be "simultaneously attracted by their poetic beauty and intensity and repelled by their raw malevolence and strangeness".

Wilby's reference to malevolence is not without basis; Gowdie describes some seemingly heinous actions. There are, for instance, the elf arrows, constructed by the Devil and elf-boys, which Gowdie and her accomplice witches (she names many) use to shoot down their victims:

> *'... we may shoot them dead at owr pleasour. Any that ar shot be us, their sowell will goe to Hevin, bot their bodies remains with us, and will flie as horsis to us, als small as strawes'.*

Though Gowdie does express remorse at killing several people with "the arrowes quhich I gott from the divell", she demonstrates none when it comes to digging up the body of an unchristened child. Indeed some of her confessions were so grim that they were omitted from the records - the scribe's use of ellipses as a form of censorship was generous to say the least (though it's also possible that they simply couldn't keep up with the rate of Gowdie's speech). Such omissions are desperately unfortunate for both scholars of the time period and those modern day witches who make use of Gowdie's confessions to guide their own magical practices.

In many senses her four confessions, made between the 13th April and 27th May 1662, form something of a grimoire of magical belief and what we can even describe, according to scholars such as Wilby and Carlo Ginzburg, as shamanic practices. Historically grimoires, particularly of the medieval period, have been written by male magicians in positions of power. In the case of Gowdie , however - as in the case of Biddy Early - we have records of the magic of common people, and in particular, the magic of common women. Wilby succinctly describes the way in which shamanic practices and experiences are specific, and often at odds with our Western propensity for psychologising, and the resultant quests for personal empowerment:

> *'The shaman enters into visionary experience in the belief that the actions he performs there will produce real, visible outcomes in the physical world [...] In the West, by contrast, the cultivation of visionary experience is predominantly concerned with psychological outcomes.'*

It is possible that Gowdie was in fact a shaman, engaging in spirit quests by means of her 'double', or spirit body. Wilby goes on to explain the way in which such practices might have made sense to Gowdie within the context of her experiences and understanding of the Kirk:

> *'...Isobel created a hybrid belief that enabled her to adhere to the Christian view, promulgated from the pulpit, that we have a spiritual soul that ascends to heaven on death while still retaining the folkloric beliefs about roving subtle bodies that underpinned popular conceptions surrounding walking spirits of the dead and existence of fairyland.'*

When it comes to fairyland - the dwelling place of the Good Neighbours - Gowdie claimed to know the place well, and spoke of entering into fairy hills where she met with their Queen:

> *'I was in the Downie-hills, got meat ther from the Qwein of Fearrie, more than I could eat. The Qwein of Fearrie is brawlie clothed in whyt linens, and in whyte and browne clothes'*

As this quote demonstrates, there is once again a consistent level of attention to detail: whether she's yarning about the colour of the Fairy

Queen's clothing or the size of the Devil's penis, a coven comprising thirteen, or night flight, Gowdie never fails to paint an exquisitely expansive picture for her audience. It seems very likely, in light of this, that Gowdie was describing scenes that had occurred in her mind's eye. Like Biddy Early, we could say that she "knew things". Beyond this, we could say that she "did things"; things such as shooting murderous elf-arrows. Wilby, in reference to Gowdie's more deadly and dangerous practices, her *maleficium*, suggests that such rites might in fact have been a twisted sort of service to the community; to, "gain valuable knowledge of those who were about to die ..." In this sense, many of Gowdie's exploits could be seen, Wilby argues, as a sort of shamanistic death-divination. Ethnographer Éva Pócs elaborates on *maleficium* as sorcery that "induced and released community tensions and conflicts." Could it be that Gowdie was in fact offering some incongruous form of healing to those around her?

To ascertain this we need to take a closer look at Gowdie's personality, though as Wilby points out, the findings shall never be crystal clear:

> *'With regards to Isobel's character and temperament, the evidence can be interpreted in contrasting ways. We can see her as aggressive and malicious, roasting clay images of innocent children before fires and nonchalantly shooting people at her "pleasur". Or we can see her as brave and self-empowered, seeking to heal and defend herself and her community through magical means [...] Or we can have her falling, as so many dark shamans seem to fall, somewhere in-between these two extremes.'*

What we do know is that Gowdie was, like Sybil Leek, shameless in the best possible sense of the word. Though we may know little about her ending - whether she was murdered following the trial, or released due to mental instability - we do know that she was fearless in the face of her likely death.

So many innocent women were murdered as witches, to the point where the words "woman" and "witch" became synonymous. Rather than stating that all the women who were killed were "innocent" of witchcraft, we might better serve and represent our contemporary spiritual communities by reminding ourselves that some of the women killed were very much "guilty" of witchcraft. And so the atrocities which took place were twofold: we lost women who were not witches *and* we lost women who were witches. Let us forget neither, for their sakes and our own.

Section Two

Practices

Banishing the Hungry Ghost
Inspired by Margot Adler

For Margot Adler, vampirism lurks in the form of each age's horror. In the present day, we find ourselves living under capitalism, an oppressive force insidiously multiplied by a hunger for resources. Our key resource being, of course, oil. As an ode to Margot Adler, and primarily to Earth itself, we might develop a practice of becoming more mindful of our own use of oil. In this culture, it is impossible to avoid consumption of oil but we can seek out oil-free products and learn to give thanks to those products we use which contain oil. For example: clothing, toiletries, vehicles, candles. The list is, tragically, endless.

We might wish to use a spell to deepen the liberation of oil. Pour around 50ml olive oil into a cup on a Sunday, the predominant culture's deigned day of rest. Stir the oil anti-clockwise, three times (for three is the problem-solver, and anti-clockwise is the direction of dissidence). As you do so, firmly say aloud the following words:

MAY ALL OILS THAT ARE ABUSED UNDER CAPITALISM BE LIBERATED FROM THEIR SERVITUDE AND ALLOWED TO REST IN THE GROUND.

Drink the olive oil to seal the command, noting how the liquid both lubricates and chokes you.

The Practice of Oomancy
Inspired by Marjorie Cameron

In Cameron's self portrait *Black Egg,* we see the artist gently clutching, just beyond her heartspace, a quintessential magical object - the egg. Of course the egg is not an object, it is a living vessel, a container for forthcoming life. Akin to the alchemist's athanor - a digesting furnace able to maintain a steady heat for a long duration - the egg is nurtured by its mother's bodily heat. The birthing hen sits upon her egg and waits as it feeds itself, building resources and coming into being by consuming its surroundings. Cameron, too, consumed her surroundings and digested them through her art. She maintained an ongoing, ever-renewing process. She had forward motion. She died at the ripe old age of 73. Despite her apparently hedonistic lifestyle, Cameron nourished herself and most nourishingly of all, always engaged in the central process of life-digestion. This is the work of the egg.

Divination using an egg features in many magical traditions and folk practices from across the globe. It is known as oomancy. If you'd like to give this a try, use the following practice to get started. It is a curse-breaking ritual; something anyone who has lived a life needs in their back pocket.

Roll an egg all over your body, inch by inch. Focus especially on the armpits, groin and under the soles of the feet. Be careful not to crack the shell despite using a firm touch of certainty. Notice as the warmth of the egg increases. Focus on the absorption of energies from your body into the egg and keep the motion rolling rather than sweeping. Having achieved the full coverage of your body, wrap the egg in a length of black fabric, ideally silk, and leave it in a safe place to gestate overnight.

The next day, unwrap the egg from its blanket and crack it open into a bowl of hot water. Widen your gaze as you look at the shapes formed by the yellow yolk and white albumen. Within the yolk is the heart and intention of the curse, as well as who cast it.

What do you see?

Within the albumen is the shape the curse took upon you. Watch it shrivel and shrink.

What do you see?

Spend some time with your body, tending to it, caring for it. Notice how you feel on the level of the physical, of thought, of emotion. Go easy.

Kinship Candle Ritual
Inspired by Doreen Valiente

Ever keen to keep witchcraft moving forwards and fit for future generations, in 1978 Doreen Valiente included a new *Liber Umbrarum* (Book of Shadows) in her publication *Witchcraft for Tomorrow*. This guide includes The Rite for Self-Initiation, a working geared towards modern solitary witches who would like to formally enter the path of witchcraft and affirm their commitment to its study and practice. In a similar vein to this rite, the following ritual is inspired by Doreen's desire to unite those of spiritual persuasions, and invokes kinship amongst witches; past, present, and future.

Begin by preparing a magical anointing blend: in a small vessel, swirl a tablespoon of olive oil together with five drops of orange essential oil and two drops of bergamot essential oil. Inhale the glorious smell of summer's sociality. Orange has a sprightly, warm character, so to match the oil's scent place a small orange-coloured candle in a suitable holder upon a windowsill where the sun shines brightly. Using the tip of a key, carve a circle into the candle to symbolise friendship and fellow- feeling.

To anoint the candle, dip your finger into the magical oil and dab some on the tip of the candle, smearing it around the wick. Sprinkle a tiny amount of dried thyme on top for its protective properties.

As you light the candle, meditate upon the flame, staring deeply into it and feeling your heart beat and flutter each time it rises and falls and crackles. Send your wishes for kinship with all witches into the heart of that flame, feeling those wishes burn in its fiery heat and grow ever greater, ever more expansive. Visualise the flame's edges spreading out into the world, bringing warmth to your fellow witches across the globe, and beyond this realm.

When the mood strikes you, which it shall, end your meditation and dance yourself into a frenzy, declaring aloud your kinship with all witches, alive and dead. End by pausing to reflect upon your enlivened state. Drink wine or any convivial drink, savouring the sensations on your lips and in your throat. Make merry. Be merry! Allow the candle to burn to its end, having sent forth its embraces.

Zodiacal Mind Training
Inspired by Sybil Leek

Sybil Leek believed that everyone has magic inside of them, and that our current form of civilization has quashed our inherent psychic abilities and connections with the stars. Astrology took an increasingly central role in Leek's magical practice as she grew older. She published many books on the use of astrology within seemingly mundane contexts, as well as more overtly sacred ones, such as in the arena of love and sex. In terms of engaging with astrology, the very least we can do is explore our Sun sign. This is the sign of the zodiac (of which there are twelve) which the Sun passes through at the time of your birth. The system of the twelve zodiac signs derives from ancient Babylonian astrology and has become a method of charting an individual's life path based on birth date. You probably know your sign already.

A second step in engaging with astrology is to keep a lunar journal. Go outside on a clear night and identify the current phase of the moon. Spend time bathing in the orb's light, or in the pit of darkness during the period of the New Moon. Notice shifts in your physical body, mind and emotions as the moon waxes and wanes. Maintaining a journal to track these changes will help you to develop awareness of cosmic forces in the key elements of your life.

Once you feel that you have started to feel a relationship with the heavens, consider undertaking the following ritual, inspired by Leek's practices of mind training and astrological awareness.

On paper, sketch an image of your zodiacal Sun sign. This can be rough and haphazard, but be sure to include each star in the constellation and the lines which connect them to form, for example, the shape of a Scorpion (for Scorpio) or a Bull (for Taurus). Once you have your drawing, place it in front of you and widen your gaze to include not only the form of your sign, but the space around it too. Stare and stare and stare and stare. Take it all in so that when you close your eyes, the image is imprinted in your mind's eye.

From here, allow the creature or object to begin moving, to become animated and three dimensional. Notice its colour, texture, posture, smell. Use all of your senses to bring your sketch to life.

Moving closer to your new companion, bow down low and rise to stand tall again, asking the sign if it has a message for you. Perhaps your sign shall refuse, perhaps it shall speak in a garbled way, a whisper, a shout, a shriek, or silently by means of a psychic connection. Thank the sign's spirit and move away without turning your back.

Step back into your physical body and open your eyes. Shake your body to dispel the sign's spirit fully, to dismiss it for now, and ponder your message. Perhaps it doesn't make any sense to you right now, but try writing it down on a slip of paper which you can place under your pillow at night. Patience, in magic as in life, is precious.

Unglamouring Ritual
Inspired by Madeline Montalban

A glamorous life need not be one filled with indescribable riches. A glamourous life is, rather, one defined by a taste for beauty, novelty and a lust for the ostentatious. There is a spirit of optimism that ushers glamour along. Luciferianism is itself optimistic - Lucifer shall bring light where there is darkness, liberation where there is stultification. Glamour in the old sense however - to mesmerise, to hold another under a state of illusion - is a key driving force in the world we live in today. The glamour of capitalism holds so many of us in its near-inescapable grip. And so, in order to live a glamour-ous life of our own making, we must break the spell that seems to be beautiful, but truly keeps us from beauty. It keeps us from our lust, our hunger, our capacity for the delights only found in the deepest kind of rest. A form of rest which is near-unobtainable in the global West. So. How to break the spell of capitalism? Well, rather like Cinderella and her ball, and that clock striking midnight, it is hard to sustain this spell. But it can be done, in stages, and built upon. It can be exercised like a muscle.

To begin, we must walk in the green at the beginning of Spring. This might mean perambulating a field, a park, a garden, a roadside. We are looking for something yellow, with many leaves - *Taraxacum officinalis*. Dandelion. Lion's tooth. The common dandelion is native to Europe but can be found across the Northern Hemisphere. If you are unable to find any then I'm afraid this ritual is going to be a slow burner - you might have to grow your own in a pot.

In herbal medicine, dandelion has many uses - it is a tonic and detoxifies the blood. Living under capitalism, detoxification is what we're looking for here, in all senses and applications of the word. Dandelions also happen to be nutritionally dense. They are cyclical beings - with flowers that open during the day and close for a little sleep during the night. These are all qualities we should like to adopt in our mission to break free from the glamour of capitalism.

Once you find yourself a dandelion, ask it whether it would like to help you, but be clear that this would involve plucking it from the ground. Say this out loud. No need to be shy (though even a whisper will do if, for example, you feel nervous speaking to flowers at the roadside). If the flower agrees, carefully pick it from the stem (not the root). If the flower is not keen, leave it alone and ask another.

Take the dandelion home with you, or continue *in situ* if it feels possible. Hold the dandelion in the Sun's direction, above your head, and ask the Sun to burn away all illusions, especially those relating to capitalism. Place a bowl in front of you and one by one, gently tug the petals from the flower, plopping them into your chosen vessel, each time chanting GLAMOUR, BE GONE!

After this is complete, proceed to scoop up the petals and shovel them into your mouth. Chew them into a mush, savouring their bitter taste, knowing that with each swallow you detoxify yourself from capitalism, if only for a short time. Having swallowed every last morsel, burn the remainder of the dandelion in your sink and wash up the bowl, leaving it to dry naturally.

The ritual is complete.

A Simple *Sabbath Unguent*
Inspired by Rosaleen Norton

Magic is, above all, relational. Like Rosaleen Norton, we work in tandem with not only humans but with animals, plants, places and - of course - spirits. All of this requires making leaps over the hedge and into the unknown worlds of risk and chaos. All of this requires energy, and of course a vehicle can help things along too. One such vehicle is the sabbath unguent, or flying ointment.

Flying ointment recipes have been traced back to the Early Modern period. Typically these balms were hallucinogenic, and were known to assist witches on their psychedelic broomstick rides across the hedge. Common ingredients include henbane, belladonna and mandrake root. The following flying ointment recipe is not hallucinogenic, but its chief ingredients - mugwort (*artemisia vulgaris*) and wormwood (*artemisia absinthium*) - are mildly psychoactive and will boost any journeying or spirit flight that you wish to undertake. Do not ingest the ointment, and do not use if you are pregnant. Use this basic recipe as a starting point for further explorations.

Stuff the largest jar you own one third full with dried mugwort and pour grapeseed oil over the top until the jar is almost full. Seal, shake and store away from direct sunlight. Repeat this process with the wormwood. Leave the herbs to brew for at least one moon cycle, shaking intermittently whilst charging them with your intention for their use, or perhaps whispering some loving words to a spirit you intend to attempt contact with. When the potions are ready, strain the herbs from the oil using cheesecloth or an extremely fine sieve.

For this recipe you shall need around half a cup of each oil. Pour the combined cupful into a *bain marie* along with two tablespoons of beeswax pellets. Melt slowly, take off the heat and add twenty drops of clary sage essential oil (for focus and calm). Working quickly, distribute the mixture into suitable clean containers and leave until cooled and set before use.

When you are ready in your ritual space, apply a teaspoon of the ointment to the soles of your feet and smear any leftovers remaining on your hands under your armpits. The absorption time can be up to an hour so be careful where you tread. Take this time to arrange your sacred space along with offerings to the spirits you wish to contact, as well as offerings to your spirit guides in exchange for their protection and companionship. Prepared, you may now settle down into a comfortable seated or supine posture and begin your journey.

The Arrival Exercise
Inspired by Mirra Alfassa

The yoga of Mirra Alfassa and her magical partner, Sri Aurobindo, has a lofty aim indeed; that of evolution, divine love and perfection. Their method - Integral Yoga - is wildly different from the yoga practices so keenly adopted in the West. Indeed, it features no physical postures (*asana*) at all. Instead, the focus is turned inwards, to that place where we can begin to comprehend the divine within. The personal nature of God can be found stored within our hearts, bodies and minds. This is the teaching of Mirra Alfassa. For Westerners, wrapped in narratives of shame and personal lack, turning within to seek the divine can be difficult, so in this practice we shall use our bodies. Not through adopting a posture, but through adopting a breathing pattern.

Find a comfortable seated position. Take a moment to arrive, to settle into your body and to bring your attention to any areas of tension, without trying to alter or correct them, without making up stories about why such tensions exist. Hold the straw between your lips, allowing your jaw to gently release so that your grip isn't too tight. Exhale gently through the straw, squeezing all the breath out of your belly, lungs and throat. Try not to strain or be forceful here; be meticulous instead.

Take a regular inhale through your nose, without the straw, and then again blow into the straw as you exhale.

Repeat this pattern slowly for about three minutes, by which time you will have found a deep sense of peace. It is from this place that we can begin to engage with our inner perfection. Perform this action once a day for maximum benefit. This is a long term process: don't get lazy. Mirra Alfassa was never lazy.

Learn the difference between lazy and relaxed.

They are not the same.

A Beginner's Guide to Possession
Inspired by Maya Deren

𝔉or the sorceress there is both an active and passive principal. We must adopt the position of both Seeker and Vessel. Spirit possession is a sphere which is riddled with terror, darkness and madness, should we be unprepared. Of course, nothing can fully prepare us, not really, for any act of magic. But we can take baby steps to work towards moving into the space where possession can happen.

Mirrors appear in much of Maya Deren's work, not least in the way she utilises a camera. And so it is with a mirror we shall begin. Use a hanging or standing mirror; one which does not require that you steady it with your hand or body. It must be the size of your face or larger. Make sure that you are in a private space and will not be disturbed or overheard.

Begin with your hair. If you have blonde hair say "I have blonde hair". If you have brown hair say, "I have brown hair". Name the thing. And then name it better: say "you have blonde/brown hair". Next, to the eyes: name their colour, describe them in more detail perhaps, in the first person. Follow this with a description in the third person. *I* becomes *you* over time. Repeat this exercise utilising your whole face as a set of talking points until you experience a state of Self/Not Self. This shall be existentially confusing but do not overthink it.

Practice doing this every day for a week, going into more and more detail every time and extending the length of your sessions. After every practice clap your hands together fiercely to re-integrate and then continue with your day.

Tarot for Creative Blocks
Inspired by Pamela Colman Smith

Pamela Colman Smith was a fervent and prolific artist, but we can imagine that even she had fallow creative periods. Invoking her verve, I invite you to work with the tarot spread below whenever you feel your creative flow is blocked or stagnant. As an appropriate ode to Pamela's book *Susan and the Mermaid*, we shall sink deeply into oceanic metaphor.

Light a candle for the artists, musicians, writers and other creatives within your ancestral lineage, whether they are related by blood or otherwise. Call them forth as you watch the flame settle into itself. If you have some, burn incense which induces a state of relaxation and heightened sensation - I find the rusty quality of Dragon's Blood helpful. Take several deep, long breaths in and out to ground yourself. Let your legs be heavy and loose.

Now, shuffle the tarot deck and randomly select six cards, which you will lay out face down upon the floor in the configuration pictured. Take several more deep breaths and imagine a wave rising from the cards and spraying droplets of water upon your damp body. Use each prompt below in turn and flip one card at a time. Spend several minutes with each card: peer into the images until they dissolve, let the freeflow of your imagination overpower you.

Write down your stream of thoughts on a piece of paper. Once you have completed this ritual, find a body of water near your home and scrunch up the paper, throwing it as far into the watery realms as is physically possible.

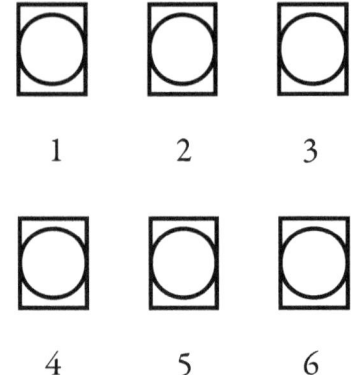

1: The weather at sea
2: The pirates besieging you
3: The cargo worthy of protection
4: Your ship's weapons
5: The land you truly seek
6: A map from the merfolk to guide you there

Your Ears Can Be Microphones
Inspired by Maria de Naglowska

Maria de Naglowska envisions a "life liberated from the prison of the flesh", using the body as a vehicle of the sacred, ecstatic magic that lies deep within us. The sex magical practices she describes are potent in part because of the manner in which they challenge deeply ingrained patterns of shame. Shame is, ultimately, a problem of the head. The following exercise helps us to overcome the problematic nature of our shame-brains by engaging with the head in a new way: as a vessel for sound. This is somewhat in tune with Naglowska's own practice of sitting in Church and hearing the sounds, the liturgy for example, but without engaging with them. The ears become microphones for divine racket, and in doing so, the incessant narratives of shame we carry, those voices and whispers that whirl around inside our skulls, become less crunchy, less overbearing. It might be easiest to record yourself reading the instructions below so that you can focus your attention on the task in hand.

Take a moment to find a comfortable seated position, or if this is not available to you, lie down with a cushion or pillow beneath your head.

Feel the points of contact between the body and the chair or ground. Allowing gravity to work upon you. Listening to the sounds inside your body, the sounds inside the room, the sounds outside the room, as they wash over you. Allowing yourself to bathe in these sounds. Searching for where the sounds inside the body meet the sounds outside the body.

Where do the sounds inside the body meet the sounds outside the body?

Allowing the tongue to rest gently behind the teeth as we open our ears, receiving sounds without straining to try and figure out where they're coming from. Taking them as they are.

It is as if there is a natural orchestra surrounding you, playing just for you. Keeping the face loose, the jaw unclenched, the eyes melting into their sockets, bringing a gentle smile to your lips.

Extending your attention outwards. Feeling the whole body bathing in the soundtrack, the soundtrack of the moment. This moment. Feel the sounds massaging your body, vibrating through your tissues, bones, organs. Taking the sounds as they come, without labelling them or getting carried away by any one sound. Your focus is wide, yet gentle and full of ease. Staying present with the sounds as they are, washing over you, washing over you.

The breath is natural, not forced or manipulated in any way. Feel your whole body vibrating with the music of your environment.

When you are ready, clap your hands twice and return.

PRACTICES

Hexing 101: Know Your Enemy
Inspired by Annie Besant

Many of the women featured in this book were involved in liberation work; fighting against institutions which sought to narrow or eradicate their rights altogether. Though Annie Besant changed her mind repeatedly when it came to her spiritual life - often guided by her head as much as her heart - in her political convictions she largely remained constant and formidably forceful. In 1877, Besant, along with Charles Bradlaugh, published a book about birth control titled *Fruits of Philosophy* (authored by Charles Knowlton). Besant and Bradlaugh were arrested on libel charges due to the fact that the distribution of written materials regarding reproduction were outlawed at that time. Initially found guilty and sentenced to six months in prison, the case was thrown out following their appeal, thanks to technical errors. Besant's proximity to prison, all too common amongst the women documented in these pages, demonstrates the way in which political causes mattered more to her than her freedom as an individual. This attitude - of collective liberation over freeing just the self - is a motif in many world religions.

There is a trend, in the contemporary occult scene, especially amongst the more popular and youthful fringes, towards political hexes: hexing the patriarchy being a predominant adage. Now, even for seasoned occultists, the patriarchy is a vast and powerful entity to reckon with. As with everything, we must walk before we can run. Annie Besant, throughout her career, argued for the benefits of education and the dissemination of information. To engage head on with malevolence then a vast amount of information on the enemy is necessary.

This ritual is a simple one: engage with independent media sources. Curate a daily ritual, against your desires to find peace, of reading about what is happening in the human world's political arena. This will be harder than it sounds, especially if you are to begin forming genuine opinions of your own rather than parroted versions of secondhand versions of thirdhand versions of hearsay. And then, begin starting to have political debates (perhaps even arguments!) with the ones you love. When you are looking out for them they will arise naturally - do not feel you need to seek these moments out by manoeuvring things to make them happen. They shall happen. And you shall be prepared. And then you will begin your training in the courts of magic.

PRACTICES

Scrying Musical Notation
Inspired by Leila Waddell

By all accounts Leila Waddell was a prodigious musician, skilled at improvisation and reading *between* lines of musical notation to discover the heart of a composition. Whether you can read musical notation or not, scrying sheet music is a wonderful way to divine, especially when it comes to matters of the heart. After all, musicality is the lifeblood of our emotions, and the harmony of the spheres can be our best guides.

To begin, procure a sheet of notation - perhaps a particular composition appeals to you, perhaps your choice is random, or based upon availability. Charity or thrift shops are a great place to unearth these treasures.

Place the sheet on a flat, plain surface such as a table or an unpatterned bedsheet. Peer over the sheet, staring as hard as you can until the black notes and lines become a blur. Ask your question aloud, with politeness but also a commanding attitude. Then loosen your gaze, widen it as far as you can and begin reading, from left to right, top to bottom, paying attention to how the notes rise and fall and the page becomes more or less crowded, or perhaps if you are trained you will be able to sight-read the melody. Let your heart rise and fall in tune with the notes, listening in your chest whilst gazing with your eyes. How do your emotions correspond to the question?

Continue until you reach the end of the music. By then you will have your answer.

A Practice for Life
Inspired by Moina Mathers

Moina Mathers offers us a lesson in doing what needs to be done, whether that means joining the war effort or stepping into a leadership role in the wake of her husband (and magical partner)'s death. There is a dialogue around "sacrifice" in the magical world, as if every aspect of our lives must be sacrificial, especially when we move in the realms of art and creative output. Perhaps we'd do better to consider the meaning of "what needs to be done" and stop making such a fuss about turning our attention to what matters, deciphering what we're willing to give up and deciding what we need to slough off and what we need to gain.

One practice to help us is to simply leave a glass of water out for other spirits every night. Refill the glass with fresh water daily and every time you place it down (on an altar, a sideboard, a table - it matters not) say, THIS IS FOR YOU, WITH WARM WISHES. Don't make up stories about the spirits this is for, or what the water might mean to them, or why you are leaving this offering. Just do the thing. Fill the glass. Put it out. Empty the glass the next day. Refill the glass. Put it out. Do what needs to be done.

PRACTICES

Ritual Towards Liberation
Inspired by Sojourner Truth

Sojourner Truth understood more deeply than most of us can imagine that we live amidst a complex web of systems and impositions; dictats which we must both abide by and have no option but to attempt to abolish, even in the tiniest of ways. We each have the possibility within us for living with wisdom, but that wisdom is typically rendered useless within the small corners of our lives. To reclaim our wisdom - our truth - is a life's work. Sojourner Truth lived her wisdom, from an early age. She demonstrated that it is neither too late nor too early to do this. The time is always this moment, in this life, in this inkling of despair, this droplet of hope.

For this ritual, find the thing within you - the inkling of despair - and identify its type as if you were a botanist classifying a plant. Look at the shape of it, the colourings, the petals. The number of them and the shape of the plant's leaves. Size up to this despair and take its number. Look at your pain squarely in its eyes and, holding a rock in your left hand, push all of that despair into the rock. Squeeze the agony, whether it be love-sickness, money worries, mental or physical illness, structural racism, sexism - whatever it is, big or small - squeeze it into the rock.

Take the rock down to the sea. Feel the weight of it, keeping it firmly in your left hand, your fingers sealed around it. Continue to squeeze. Transfer the rock to your right hand , saying the words I TRANSFER MY PAIN TO THIS ROCK. Throw the rock, as far as you can, out into the water, yelling PAIN I EXPEL YOU. Turn your back on the sea and do not look behind you as you walk away. Say the following words, or similar, under your breath: PAIN, OH PAIN, IF ONLY IT WERE THAT EASY. IF I COULD TAKE YOU TO

THE BEACH AND TOSS YOU INTO THE SEA ALL WOULD BE RIGHT. AS IT IS NOT, AND AS THERE IS ALWAYS MORE PAIN, I VOW TO FIGHT FOR LIBERATION.

Repeat this ritual every time you feel overwhelmed, disengaged, complacent or dull. Take your endless pain out into the world. Never leave it behind, not until the last drop is gone (even if that takes forever).

PRACTICES

Ancestral Altar in a Box
Inspired by Marie Laveau

Marie Laveau's lavish personal altars were often described as being hidden in her house by a curtain. Whilst this requires possibilities for fitting interior design, there is a simpler method of keeping your altar private. There are many reasons to create an altar in a box: privacy, lack of space, containment. But ultimately, when it comes to ancestral work, for boundaries' sake.

Storing keepsakes in a box is a technique old as time & for good reason! Ancestral work is arduous, draining, alluring, addictive. Calling upon our dead is a weighty business & does not leave us untouched or necessarily healed.

Creating an ancestral altar box enables you to close the lid on these undertakings when you need to turn back towards life, which you must do for the sake of not just your sanity, but for love of the living and of life itself.

Eyebright Tea
Inspired by Biddy Early

Euphrasia salisburgensis - Irish eyebright - is a declining species of the already rare plant eyebright. Known locally as *Glanrosc gaelach*, it is now confined to western Ireland, and most abundant in County Clare - the home of Biddy Early. Like other species of *Euphrasia* in the UK, Irish eyebright is semi-parasitic; it is attached to and somewhat dependent upon the roots of its host plant for nutrients. As it is an annual, however, any damage is within limits. This community-loving plant needs others, but it won't drink them completely dry. The white and yellow flowers seem to reach forth like hands, offering their gifts which, unsurprisingly, generally relate to matters of sight. A traditional remedy for runny hayfever eyes, conjunctivitis and other eye-related maladies, distilled eyebright juice would often be mixed with ale or wine and either taken orally or dropped directly into the eyes.

Eyebright has magical qualities too; it supports psychic skills and inner vision. Try filling a pouch with dried eyebright (it needn't be the Irish variant!) and carrying it on your person. Alternatively make a simple eyebright tea to drink regularly. Steep two teaspoons of the herb in a cup of boiling water for around seven minutes to brew.

PRACTICES

Witch Bottle for Bravery
Inspired by Isobel Gowdie

In 17th century East Anglia, stoneware bottles or jugs were traditionally created by cunning folk, astrologers or chemists as counter-spells or 'prepared cures' to retaliate against suspected witchcraft. Folklorist Icy Sedgwick recalls the story of cunningman James Murrell of Essex, who used a cast iron witch bottle to counter a curse placed on a young woman. He reportedly held the bottle in a blazing fire until the witch appeared and begged him desperately to stop. The next day, the girl was found to have miraculously recovered, whilst the witch had burned to a crisp.

Over 100 witch bottles, mostly from the 17th to 19th centuries, have been unearthed in the UK alone - under houses, in ditches, streams, and graveyards. Typical burial sites were in chimneys or under hearths - evil spirits were thought to enter houses via such thresholds. Last year, a Victorian glass bottle was discovered at the site of the former Star and Garter Inn in Northamptonshire. It contained fish hooks, human teeth, glass, and liquid (urine and other bodily fluids have long been typical ingredients). The inn happened to be the 1761 birthplace of Angeline Tubbs, the infamous Witch of Saratoga. We might wonder whether the bottle's creator was guarding against some of Angeline's lingering forces.

The following basic witch bottle will conjure bravery, adventurousness, and wondrous naivety as you set out on any journey. It'll also keep you safe, which is important given all that naivety and innocence.

Firstly, cleanse your jar by washing it thoroughly then placing it upside down on a lined baking tray (newspaper works just fine as a liner). Bake it in the oven on a very low heat for 15 minutes. Leave to cool. You can wash the lid too but no need to bake it.

Quarter fill your container with lavender, an abundant and famed soother of nerves. Next add an anise pod and a sprig of rosemary (for passion and purity of intention), plus the small feather of any bird. This will keep you soaring high. A rusty nail or piece of metal gives strength and helps to banish countering forces. Bent rusty nails were thought to be especially potent for this purpose.

Top up with a clear spirit such as gin or vodka, to keep you giddy with a lust for life. Use candle wax (ideally a fiery red or orange) to thoroughly seal.

Bibliography

Chapter One: Margot Adler

Adler, M. (1979) *Drawing Down the Moon*; Penguin Books.

Adler, M. (1998) *Heretic's Heart: A Journey through Spirit and Revolution*; Beacon Press.

Adler, M. (2014) *Vampires are Us: Understanding Our Love Affair with the Immortal Dark Side*; Red Wheel/ Weiser.

Hutton, R. (1990) *The Triumph of the Moon: A History of Modern Witchcraft*; Oxford University Press.

Chapter Two: Doreen Valiente

Heselton, Philip (2016) *Doreen Valiente Witch*; Centre for Pagan Studies.

Hutton, R. (1990) *The Triumph of the Moon: A History of Modern Witchcraft*; Oxford University Press.

Valiente, D. (1962) *Where Witchcraft Lives*; Aquarian.

Valiente, D. (1973) *An ABC of WItchcraft Past & Present*; Robert Hale.

Valiente, D. (1975) *Natural Magic*; Robert Hale.

Valiente, D. (1978) *Witchcraft for Tomorrow*; Robert Hale.

Valiente D. (1989) *The Rebirth of Witchcraft*; Robert Hale.

BIBLIOGRAPHY

Chapter Three: Marjorie Cameron

Cameron, M. & Parsons, J. (2014) *Songs for the Witch Woman*; Fulgur Press.

Hedenborg White, M. (2019) *The Eloquent Blood: The Goddess Babalon and the Construction of Femininities in Western Esotericism*; Oxford University Press.

Kansa, S. (2014) *Wormwood Star: The Magickal Life of Marjorie Cameron*; Mandrake of Oxford.

Pendle, G. (2005) *Strange Angel: The Otherworldly Life of Rocket Scientist John Whiteside Parsons*; Weidenfeld & Nicholson.

Grey, P. (2011) *The Two Antichrists*; Scarlet Imprint.

Chapter Four: Sybil Leek

Hutton, R. (1990) *The Triumph of the Moon: A History of Modern Witchcraft;* Oxford University Press.

Leek, S. (1964) *A Shop in the High Street*; D. McKay Co.

Leek, S. (1968) *Diary of a Witch*; Signet Books.

Leek, S. (1972) *My Life in Astrology*; Signet Books.

Leek, S. (1975) *Complete Art of Witchcraft Penetrating the Mystery behind Magic Powers*; Leslie Frewin.

Valiente D. (1989) *The Rebirth of Witchcraft*; Robert Hale.

Chapter Five: Madeline Montalban

Howard, M. (2010) *Modern Wicca: A History from Gerald Gardner to the Present Day*; Llewellyn.

Howard, M. (2016), 'Teachings of the Light: Madeline Montalban and the Order of the Morning Star', *The Luminous Stone: Lucifer in Western Esotericism*, ed. Howard, M. & Schulke, D.A.; Three Hands Press.

Montalban, M. (1983) *Prediction Book of the Tarot*; Blandford Press.

Phillips, J. (2012) *Madeline Montalban: The Magus of St. Giles* (Neptune Press, 2nd edition).

Phillips, J. (2021) 'Madeline Montalban: Magus of the Morning Star', *Essays on Women in Western Esotericism*, ed. Hale, A.; Palgrave Macmillan.

Valiente D. (1989) *The Rebirth of Witchcraft*; Robert Hale.

Chapter Six: Rosaleen Norton

Drury, N. (2016) *Pan's Daughter: The Magical World of Rosaleen Norton* (revised & expanded); Mandrake of Oxford

Norton, R. (2009) *Thorn in the Flesh: A Grim-memoire*; Teitan Press.

Valiente, D. (1973) *An ABC of WItchcraft Past & Present*; Robert Hale.

Valiente D. (1989) *The Rebirth of Witchcraft*; Robert Hale.

The Witch of King's Cross (2001) [Film] dir. Sonia Bible; Journeyman Pictures.

Chapter Seven: Mirra Alfassa

Alfassa, M. (2003[1978]) *Collected Works of the Mother* (Volumes 1-17); Sri Aurobindo Ashram

Godwin, J., Chanel, C. & Deveney, J. (1995) *The Hermetic Brotherhood of Luxor: Initiatic & Historical Documents of an Order of Practical Occultism*; Samuel Weiser.

Joshi, K. (1989 [1996]) *Sri Aurobindo & The Mother: Glimpses of Their Experiments, Experiences and Realisations*; The Mother's Institute of Research.

Julich, S. L. (2013) 'A New Creation on Earth: Death & Transformation in the Yoga of Mother Mirra Alfassa', *Integral Review*, 9 (3).

Kuchuk, N. (2023) 'The life incarnate & the life divine: spiritual evolution, androgyny & the face of the goddess in the teachings of Mirra Alfassa, the Mother of Integral Yoga', *Studies in Religion/ Sciences Religieuses*, 52 (1).

Van Vreckhem, G. (2004 [2011]) *The Mother: The Story of Her Life*; Rupa Publications.

Chapter Eight: Maya Deren

Deren, M. (1953[2004]) *Divine Horsemen: The Living Gods of Haiti*; Documentext

Deren, M. (2004) *Essential Deren: Collected Writings on Film,* ed. McPherson, B.; Documentext.

Keller, S. (2014) *Maya Deren: Incomplete Control*; Columbia University Press.

Nichols, B (ed.) (2001) *Maya Deren & the American Avant Garde*; University of California Press.

Noble, J. (2019) 'Maya Deren: The Magical Woman as Filmmaker'; *Frames Cinema Journal*, Issue 16.

Noble, J. (2017) 'Clear Dreaming: Maya Deren, Surrealism & Magic', *Surrealism, Occultism and Politics: In Search of the Marvellous*, ed. Bauduin, T. M. et al.; Routledge.

Chapter Nine: Pamela Colman Smith

Kaplan, S. R. (2018) *Pamela Colman Smith: The Untold Story*; U.S. Games.

Ransome, A. (1907 [2014]) *Bohemia in London*; Nabu Press.

Waite, A.E. (1938 [2016]) *Shadows of Life and Thought: the Autobiography of A.E. Waite*; Bardic Press.

Robinson, D. (2020) *Pamela Colman Smith - Tarot Artist -* The Pious Pixie, Fonthill Media.

BIBLIOGRAPHY

Chapter Ten: Maria de Naglowska

Alexandrian, S. (2015) *The Great Work of the Flesh: Sexual Magic East and West*; Destiny Books.

DeSpencer, M. (2016) 'Lucifer in La Ville Lumière', *The Luminous Stone: Lucifer in Western Esotericism*, ed. Howard, M. & Schulke, D.A.; Three Hands Press.

Naglowska, M. (2011) *Advanced Sex Magic: The Hanging Mystery Initiation*; Inner Traditions.

Naglowka, M. (2011) *The Light of Sex: Initiation, Magic & Sacrament*; Inner Traditions.

Naglowska, M. (2013) *Initiatic Eroticism: And Other Occult Writings from La Flèche*; Inner Traditions.

North, R. (2011) *The Illustrated Grimoire of Maria de Naglowska*; Lulu.

Olzi, Michele (2019) 'From Russia with Love, a Case of Russian Culture and Immigration in Western Esotericism', *Studies on Western Esotericism in Central and Eastern Europe* (Studies in Cultural Iconology 1), N. Radulović, K. M. Hess (ed.). University of Szeged, JATEPress.

Sowerwine, C. (2001) *France Since 1870: Culture, Politics and Society*; Palgrave MacMillan.

Urban, H. (2021) *Secrecy: Silence, Power, and Religion* (University of Chicago Press).

Chapter Eleven: Annie Besant

Besant, A. (1885) *Annie Besant: An Autobiography*; in public domain.

Besant, A. (1894) *Building of the Cosmos & Other Lectures*; Delhi Open Books.

Besant, A. (1897 [2008]) *The Ancient Wisdom*; Prabhat Books.

Blavatsky (1888 [2015]) *The Secret Doctrine*; Theosophy Trust.
Lachman, G. (2012) *Madame Blavatsky: The Mother of Modern Spirituality*; Penguin.

Singh, C. L. (2019) 'Annie Besant's Defence of the Indian Caste System: A Critique', *History & Sociology of South Asia*, 13 (1).

Strube, J. (2021) 'Theosophy, Race, and the Study of Esotericism', *Journal of the American Academy of Religion*, 89 (4).

Chapter Twelve: Leila Waddell

Booth, M. (2000) *A Magick Life: The Biography of Aleister Crowley*; Coronet Books.

Brown, J. (1978) 'Aleister Crowley's Rites of Eleusis', *The Drama Review*, 22(2), 3-26

Crowley, A. (1910) 'The Rites of Eleusis: Their Origin and Meaning', *The Bystander*, 23rd November.

Crowley, A., Desti, M. & Waddell, L. (1913 [1997]) *Magick: Liber

ABA, Book 4, parts I-IV, 2nd revised edition; Red Wheel/ Weiser.

Gorman, A. (2019) 'Hidden Women of History: Leila Waddell: Australian violinist, philosopher of magic and fearless rebel', *The Conversation*, 24th September.

Keller, Phyllis (1971) 'George Sylvester Viereck: The Psychology of a German-American Militant', *Journal of Interdisciplinary History*, 2:1 (Summer 1971).

King, F. X. (1977) *The Magical World of Aleister Crowley*; Littlehampton Book Services.

Tupman, T. W. (2003) *Theatre Magick: Aleister Crowley and the Rites of Eleusis*; Ohio State University.

Chapter Thirteen: Moina Mathers

Colquhoun, I. (1975) *Sword of Wisdom: MacGregor Mathers and the Golden Dawn*; G.P. Putnam's Sons.

Denisoff, D. (2014) 'Performing the Spirit: Theatre, the Occult, and the Ceremony of Isis', *Paganism in Late Victorian Britain*, August 2014.

Denisoff, D. (2022) *Decadent Ecology in British Literature and Art, 1860-1910*; Cambridge University Press.

Fortune, D. (1930 [2021]) *Psychic Self Defence*; Red Wheel/Weiser.

Fortune, D. (1930b [2000]) *The Training and Work of an Initiate*; Red Wheel/Weiser.

Greer, M. K. (1995) *Women of the Golden Dawn: Rebels and Priestesses*; Inner Traditions.

Lees, F. (1900) 'Isis Worship in Paris', *The Humanitarian*, Vol. XVI: II.

Owen, A. (2004) *The Place of Enchantment: British Occultism and the Culture of the Modern*; University of Chicago Press.

https://hermeticgoldendawn.org/the-flying-rolls.

Chapter Fourteen: Sojourner Truth

Braude, A. (1989) *Radical Spirits: Spiritualism and Women's Rights in Nineteenth-Century America*; Indiana University Press.

Johnson, P.E. & Wilentz, S. (1994 [2012]) *The Kingdom of Matthias: A Story of Sex and Salvation in 19th Century America*; Oxford University Press.

Painter, N. Irvine (1996) *Sojourner Truth: A Life, A Symbol*; W. W. Norton.

Truth, S. (1850 [2023]) *The Narrative of Sojourner Truth*; SeaWolf Press.

Truth, S. (1863 [2020]) *Ain't I A Woman?*; Penguin Classics.

Washington, M. (2011) *Sojourner Truth's America*; University of Illinois Press.

BIBLIOGRAPHY

Chapter Fifteen: Marie Laveau

Alvarado, D. (2020) *The Magic of Marie Laveau: Embracing the Spiritual Legacy of The Voodoo Queen of New Orleans*; Weiser Books.

Fandrich, I.J. (2012) *Marie Laveau: The Mysterious Voodoo Queen: A Study of Powerful Female Leadership in Nineteenth Century New Orleans*; University of Louisiana at Lafayette Press.

Long, C. M. (2006) *A New Orleans Voudou Priestess: The Legend and Reality of Marie Laveau*; University Press of Florida.

Ward, M. (2004) *Voodoo Queen: The Spirited Lives of Marie Laveau*; University Press of Mississippi.

Chapter Sixteen: Biddy Early

Gregory, A. (1920) *Visions and Beliefs in the West of Ireland*; G. P. Putnam's Sons.

Lenihan, E. (1987 [2018]) *In Search of Biddy Early (New Edition)*; Hayesprint Publishing.

Long, T. K. (1990) 'Biddy Early: The Witch of Kilbarron', *Fate*, October 1990.

Rainsford, J. (2012) 'Biddy Early's Limerick Connections', *Limerick Chronicle*, Winter 2012.

Walker-Dunseith, H. M. (2022) 'The Healer in the tower: Biddy Early and discourses of healing in the work of W.B. Yeats and Lady Augusta Gregory'; *Irish Studies Review* 30:3.

Chapter Seventeen: Isobel Gowdie

Ginzburg, C. (1990) *Ecstasies: Deciphering the Witches' Sabbath*; Hutchinson Radius.

Maxwell-Stuart, P. G. (2005 [2007]) *The Great Scottish Witch-Hunt*; Tempus.

Pócs, E. (1999) *Between the Living and the Dead*; Central European University Press.

Wilby, E. (2010 [2013]) *The Visions of Isobel Gowdie: Magic, Witchcraft and Dark Shamanism in Seventeenth-Century Scotland*; Sussex Academic Press.

Ùna Maria Blyth - Shetland Isles
Photographed by Art by May Graham (21/03/2023)

Acknowledgements

Sitting here in my croft house in Shetland, it has often felt like I've been writing this book in a vacuum. That has never been true. Writing books is an incredibly lonely process, but I have not been alone.

I would firstly like to thank my witch-wife Belladonna, for reading early drafts and challenging me to be bold, to be brave, to ARGUE! You are my greatest teacher.

I would also like to thank my editor Kazim for supporting me throughout this entire process. I have been at all times delighted by your occult knowledge and deep warmth.

There are many friends whose belief in me - and my plots, plans and projects - has caught me by surprise and fuelled me. I have so much love and thanks to give to Kirsty, Andrea, Cassy, Lucy, Paulina, Laura, Bob, Celeste, Icy, Simon and Alice.

Finally, great thanks to my familiars, Theo and Nunu, for always being at the foot of the bed-office.

www.ingramcontent.com/pod-product-compliance
Lightning Source LLC
LaVergne TN
LVHW071946080526
838202LV00064B/6686